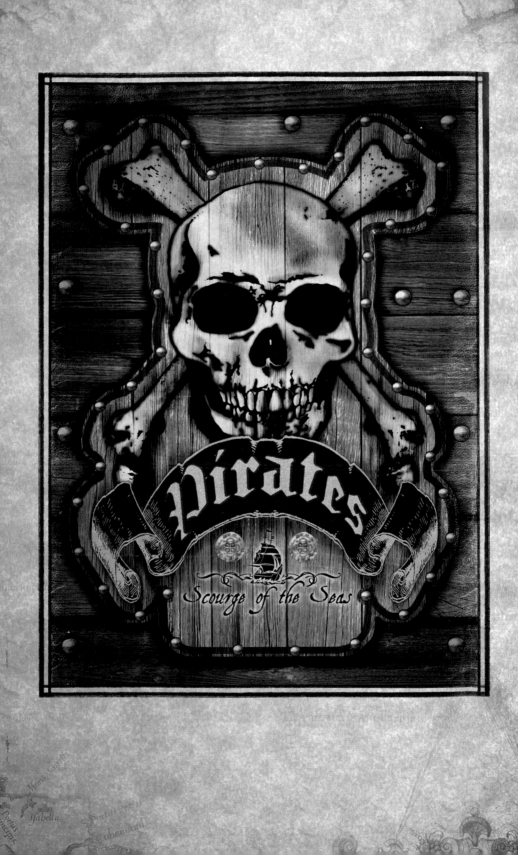

Pirates

Scourge of the Seas

John Reeve Carpenter

STERLING

New York / London
www.sterlingpublishing.com

Library of Congress Cataloging-in-Publication Data Available

1 2 3 4 5 6 7 8 9 10

Published in 2008 by Sterling Publishing Co., Inc.
387 Park Avenue South, New York, NY 10016

© 2006 JW Cappelens forlag under license from Gusto Company AS
Written by John Reeve Carpenter
Original concept by Gusto Company
Designed by Allen Boe
Illustrations, ScanPix, Getty Images, and AnnDréa Boe

Distributed in Canada by Sterling Publishing
c/o Canadian Manda Group, 165 Dufferin Street
Toronto, Ontario, Canada M6K 3h6

For information about custom editions, special sales, premium and corporate
purchases, please contact Sterling Special Sales Department at 800-805-5489
or specialsales@sterlingpub.com

Manufactured in China

Sterling ISBN: 978-1-4027-6311-3

Contents

Introduction

Buccaneer cannons boom across the water. A merchant ship reels under the hailstorm of chain shot that rips through its rigging and splinters its mast. The whistle of shrapnel scuttering through the air is matched by the harrowing screams of sea brigands as they whirl their grappling hooks above their heads.

Musket balls fly. Grenades explode. A wounded helmsman falls to the deck and the ship begins to lurch wildly as the wheel spins unchecked. Flames lick the sails as a volley of flintlocks discharge. Pirates swarm onto the deck of their prize, swinging their axes and hacking with their cutlasses. Terrified merchant seamen are cut down by sword, rapier, dagger, and dirk.

Suddenly, through the smoke a hellish vision appears – a huge hairy beast with braided rope burning in his matted hair. His dark eyes stare coldly. Blackbeard will show no mercy.

Pirates have sailed the seven seas ever since there was booty to plunder. The earliest pirates predate the pyramids and piracy still flourishes today in unstable regions of the world. Yet the image that all of us grow up with is that of the eyepatched eighteenth-

century brigand, with a peg-leg and a parrot perched on his shoulder, clutching a cutlass in one hand and a treasure map in the other. This book explores the golden age of piracy, but it broadens its sights and separates the myth from the reality.

If you are looking for exotic desert islands and sword-wielding desperadoes, they are here, but you will also learn what life was really like for the scourge of the seas: what motivated them, what kept them together, the hardships they had to endure, and the adventures they sought.

Chapter one traces the beginnings of piracy in the eastern Mediterranean and its development through the nineteenth century. Piracy has never been straightforward; the boundaries of its morality and allegiances are often blurred. One nation's hero is another nation's pirate criminal. Many pirates plundered "legally" in the name of their countries; others were innocent victims captured by pirates and forced into a life of crime. Some pirates were gentlemen who showed mercy to their captives; others were ruthless psychopaths who showed no quarter and brutally tortured and killed all those who were unfortunate enough to fall into their hands.

The second chapter explores real life aboard a pirate ship; it also looks at the unhappy fate of a regular sailor and shows why so many men were tempted into piracy. The social structure of a pirate ship was clearly defined; pirates were a much more loyal and disciplined bunch than legend has given them credit for. The pirate code of conduct was honorable; pirates looked after their own and dealt ruthlessly with any betrayal. The harsh living conditions on board ship and the pirate crew, from captain and to powder monkey, are brought vividly to life, as are the tortures that were meted out to those who transgressed, or to victims who refused to yield up their treasures.

Chapters three and four throw you into the thick of battle, describing the tactics and weapons used by pirates, as well as their clothes, flags, and the ships they sailed in. The final chapter is a rogue's gallery of over a dozen notorious pirates, from two sixteenth-century Barbary sea dog siblings to the most successful pirate who ever lived—a woman who terrorized the South China Sea in the nineteenth century.

Four appendices explore pirate language, beliefs, and superstitions. Be warned that they may blow some of your preconceptions about treasure chests, hooks, peg-legs, and parrots clean out of the water. So ahoy there matey! Batten down the hatches and weigh anchor for a voyage that will shiver your timbers and stiffen your futtock shrouds right to the bitter end.

Chapter 1

The History of Piracy

❧≈≈≈❧

Ever since there have been ships and trade, there has been piracy. However, the era of piracy that we are most familiar with today is a narrow window spanning the sixteenth and early seventeenth centuries, and the golden age of piracy, which took place between 1690 and 1730, is narrower still. The history of piracy begins as far back as ancient times.

ANCIENT PIRATES

The earliest pirates predate the pyramids. During the fourteenth century B.C., sea raiders known as the Lukka operated off the coast of Asia Minor. (It is believed that piracy in the eastern Mediterranean occurred even earlier.) The Lukka, who allied with the Hittite Empire, targeted Egyptian ships and raided Cyprus.

For the next 200 years the eastern Mediterranean was dominated by a group of maritime nomads, known collectively as the "Sea Peoples," who stifled sea trade. Inscriptions on the tomb of the Egyptian Pharaoh Rameses the Great describe how he defeated the Sea Peoples, who attacked Egypt in 1186 B.C. After this, most of the Sea Peoples settled

in Palestine. Some became the ancestors of the Philistines and Phoenicians.

Greek historians such as Herodotus have written about pirates and how Greece attempted to fight them. Mercenary pirate navies flourished in Cilicia, Illyria, the Aegean, the northeastern Adriatic, and the eastern Mediterranean. Crete was a pirate base for 800 years.

The Roman Empire managed to bring piracy under control in the biggest anti-pirate campaign of all time. In 67 B.C. Pompey used 500 ships, 120,000 Roman troops, and an enormous military budget to decimate the Cilician sea raiders and the Illyrian pirates. He rid the Mediterranean of piracy in three months, killing over 10,000 pirates and relocating many more.

Piracy in the region was crushed for 400 years, until the decline of the Roman Empire in the fifth century A.D., when it began to spread again.

MEDIEVAL PIRATES

After the fall of the Roman Empire, the Byzantine Empire protected the Mediterranean from pirates until the Empire's decline in the twelfth century. With the sacking of Constantinople in A.D. 1204, the Aegean once again became a base for pirates as the Byzantine Empire began using Aegean pirates, many of whom were Italian, to suppress Venetian and Genoese shipping.

The Muslim Ottoman Empire had neutralized the Aegean pirate communities by the fourteenth century, and enlisted corsairs to attack the maritime trade of its enemies. After the fall of the Byzantine Empire, the pro-Ottoman Barbary pirates became prominent *(see page 19)* and privateering—government contracted piracy—came into its own. European monarchs issued contracts to pirates to fight against the Moors, Turks, and pagans in response to relentless attacks against European ships and ports. European ports grouped together into alliances of trading guilds to establish trade monopolies and combat piracy. The biggest of these guilds was the Hanseatic League, which started in Lübeck and Hamburg and grew to include a total of nineteen ports. In England the League of the Cinque Ports, which was formed to protect the English Channel, itself ended up as a pirate organization, attacking any ships that weren't English. The greatest threat to the Hanseatic League was the Victual Brothers, a group of German pirates who attacked the Hanse port of Bergen in 1392; they were a constant nuisance until their capture ten years later.

Constant war between France and England during the late fourteenth and early fifteenth centuries resulted in the English Channel and the Bay of Biscay teeming with pirates and privateers, as each country sought to protect its interests by issuing "reprisal" rights to pirates. These later became the "Letter of Marque" system—government-approved piracy. Shipbuilding had advanced sufficiently to allow voyages a long way from home. As trade expanded, so did piracy.

THE BARBARY PIRATES

For 150 years, beginning in the late fifteenth century, the Barbary pirates terrorized the Mediterranean, often acting on behalf of the Ottoman Empire. Using North Africa as a base, they attacked non-Muslim European ships and looted coastal towns. They were notorious for their brutality, but they were organized very effectively by a captain's council, called the Taife Raisi, which oversaw their North African pirate bases and liaised between them, the local rulers, and the Ottoman Empire. They also helped to defend Tunis, Algiers, Tripoli, Salè, and other Barbary ports. The Taife Raisi ensured that the booty was divided effectively between the pirates and the local rulers.

Fleets of Barbary pirates also fought as part of the Ottoman navy during the sixteenth century, defending the Barbary coast against the Christians, especially the Spanish. They captured large numbers of Christian slaves from Western Europe, and sold them in slave markets in North Africa. It has been estimated that, during the sixteenth and seventeenth centuries, a total of 1,250,000 European Christian slaves suffered this fate.

The most famous Barbary pirates were the Barbarossa brothers, Aruj and Hizir Rais. They were supported by an Egyptian emir and the Sultan of Tunis, and were powerful enough to attack warships and merchant vessels from their base at Djerba, and later Djidjelli. In 1516 Aruj led an uprising against the Sultan of Algiers, killed him, and took the sultanate for himself. He defended Algiers against the Spanish and was killed at Tlemcen after a six-month siege. Hizir then joined forces with the Ottoman emperor and was officially named Sultan of Algiers. His repeated raids on Spanish interests earned him the nickname

Khair-ed-Din ("the gift of God") and he was a major factor in the Ottoman Empire gaining control of the Mediterranean.

The Barbary pirates didn't restrict themselves to the Mediterranean. In 1641, the Reverend Devereux Spratt was captured and sold into slavery while crossing the Irish Sea from County Cork to England. Writing of his ordeal he claimed that before he even lost sight of land he and his crew of 120 "were captured by Algerine pirates, who put all the men in irons." According to historian Robert Davis, "Admiralty records show that during this time the corsairs plundered British shipping pretty much at will, taking no fewer than 466 vessels between 1609 and 1616, and 27 more vessels from near Plymouth in 1625."

By the end of the sixteenth century, the Barbary Coast was a secure part of the Ottoman Empire. The Barbary pirates were in decline by the mid-seventeenth century, but they continued to operate as late as the early nineteenth century.

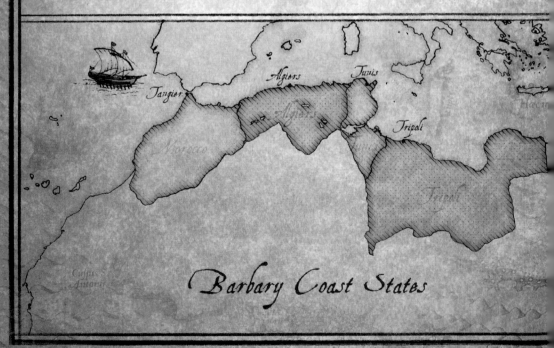

Barbary Coast States

THE KNIGHTS OF MALTA

While the Muslim Barbary pirates were operating from the North coast of Africa, the Christian Knights of Malta fought against Muslim interests in the Mediterranean. The Knights of Malta were a fervent religious order that had been given control of Malta by Emperor Charles V, and they used it as a base to fight against the Ottoman Empire with a small fleet of galleys. They also had a secondary base at Tripoli, which was lost to the Turks in 1551.

The Knights of Malta conducted pirate expeditions to raid Barbary coastal settlements and harass Muslim shipping. They also attacked Venetian shipping (much to the anger of the Pope) because the Venetians were at peace with the Ottoman Empire. Everything they plundered was taken back to their order. By the end of the 1550s, many people saw them as little more than pirates and they were held in contempt by the church. One Venetian official called them "corsairs parading crosses."

In 1565, Malta was besieged for four months by a huge Turkish fleet. The Turks took control of part of the island, destroyed nearly all of the old city, and killed half the knights. Spain sent reinforcements and the Turks retreated, marking the end of the pirating heyday of the Knights of Malta, although they continued to operate for another 200 years, until Malta surrendered to Napoleon in 1798.

THE SPANISH MAIN

Spain's colonial expansion into America began with the voyage of Christopher Columbus in 1492, and continued so that by the mid-seventeenth century it controlled a large area of the Caribbean basin which became known as the Spanish Main.

In the 1494 Treaty of Tordesillas, the Pope decreed that the Spanish and Portuguese were to divide the area outside of Europe into a duopoly along a north-south meridian (the Tordesillas line). All land discovered west of the line would belong to Spain, and all new land in the east would belong to the Portuguese.

The Spanish controlled the Caribbean until the early seventeenth century, and the huge fleets of Spanish ships that journeyed between Spain and the Spanish Main became prime targets for pirates. French and English pirates managed to form colonies in the Caribbean that were strong enough to resist being destroyed by the Spanish and they used these strongholds as bases from which to prey on Spanish shipping. The main ports in the Spanish Main were Havana, Cartagena, Vera Cruz, and Panama. All of these ports became targets of pirates, including Sir Francis Drake and Sir Henry Morgan.

The English assault on the Spanish Main was led by Sir Francis Drake, whose numerous expeditions between 1570 and 1595 were not always supported by the British crown.

By contrast, French Huguenot pirates waged war against the Spanish with the full support of the French crown. France was at war with

Haben Lector candide fortiß ac inuictiß Ducis Draeck ad viuum imaginem qui
toto terrarum orbe, duorum annorum, et mensium decem spatio, Zephiris fauen-
tibus circumduciu. Angliam soli proprias. 4. Cal Octobr. anno â partu Virgi-
nis 1580 reuisit cum antea portu soluisset 13. Decem: anni. 1577.

Spain during the sixteenth century, and refused to accept the Treaty of Tordesillas that had divided the world between Spain and Portugal. French pirates were issued with Letters of Marque that authorized them to attack Spanish ships, in return for sharing the plunder with the French government. The most damaging French attacks, which took place in the 1540s and 1550s, included the attack on Havana and the plundering and destruction of Cartagena. France and Spain made peace in 1544, but pirate raids continued, and by 1552 the two countries were at war again. Devastating French raids followed in the Canary Islands, along the coast of Hispaniola, and in the cities of Santiago and Havana. By the end of the 1550s, France had the upper hand in the Caribbean, and in 1564 French Huguenots established a pirate settlement at Fort Caroline in Florida.

The following year, King Philip II of Spain partially funded the Spanish nobleman Pedro Menéndez de Aviles and his mission to destroy the colony at Fort Caroline. Menéndez sailed from Cadiz with a fleet of thirty ships, 2,000 soldiers, and a few hundred settlers, but a storm split up the fleet, so he ultimately sailed to Florida with five ships and 600 men. He founded a colony south of Fort Caroline called St. Augustine, then marched on the French fort which was poorly defended. The French fleet sent to attack Menéndez was shipwrecked, and Menéndez captured and massacred 200 survivors. He thus almost single-handedly brought an end to organized French resistance in the Spanish Main, and was made Governor of Havana in recognition of his service to the crown.

BUCCANEERS IN THE SEVENTEENTH CENTURY

During the first half of the seventeenth century, French raiders initially operating from the island of Hispaniola (modern-day Haiti and Santa Domingo) attacked Spanish shipping in the Spanish Main. By the middle of the century there were thousands of of traders, mainly of French, Dutch, and English extraction, based at ports such as the island of Tortuga and Port Royal in Jamaica. These pirates were the buccaneers, named after the original French settlers who made a living hunting cattle and *boucanning* (smoking meat).

The Port Royal buccaneers were known as "The Brethren of the Coast," and were mainly English. Famous buccaneers include Sir Henry Morgan *(see page 125)*, François L'Olonnais *(see page 128)*, Michel de Grammont, Edward Davis, and Laurens de Graff.

The first buccaneers were tough frontiersmen who lived off the land, until Spanish attempts to get rid of them caused many to become pirates. Buccaneers attacked ships by sneaking up on them from behind, usually at night. They jammed the rudder to prevent the ship from escaping, and killed important crew members, such as the helmsmen and the officers. These lightning raids were quick and brutal; often, the Spanish crews would surrender without putting up a fight, once they realized that their ship had been overrun before they could raise the alarm.

These plundering sea rovers were made famous by the buccaneer surgeon Alexander Exquemelin, who sailed with L'Olonnais and Morgan. In his book *The Buccaneers of America*, published in 1678, he vividly recounted their exploits, their rules of conduct, and their way of life.

The Battle Between y.e Spaniards and Pirates or Buccaneers Before the City of PANAMA

In the latter part of the seventeenth century buccaneers were so numerous that they were able to mount attacks on coastal towns. They would weigh anchor and then attack further up the coast from the landward side, a tactic that Henry Morgan used to great effect.

Buccaneers were united in their hatred of Spain and formed an informal mercenary navy, offering their services to anyone who wanted to attack Spanish interests, as long as they received a share of the plunder.

By the late seventeenth century the buccaneers' sphere of influence extended way beyond the Caribbean to cover the whole of the Pacific from California to Chile. Notable buccaneer victories during this period were the capture of New Segovia on the American mainland, L'Olonnais's control of the Gulf of Venezuela, and Morgan's capture of Porto Bello and Panama. The fall of Porto Bello led to a treaty between England and Spain in the New World. England was allowed to keep all its New World holdings in return for agreeing to recognize Spain's trading monopoly. The treaty was sustained with varying degrees of success; for example, the governor of Jamaica, Thomas Modyford, had already granted Morgan permission to attack Panama. When Morgan sacked Panama in 1671, the sheer audacity and brutality of the attack inaugurated the heyday of the buccaneers, which lasted for the next fifteen years.

After 1685, the buccaneers went into decline, partly because the Spanish fleet system was waning, but also because their way of life was insecure, hand-to-mouth, and ultimately self-destructive in its profligacy and brutality. Their excesses were neatly summed up by Exquemelin: "[They spend] their gains . . . with great liberality, giving themselves freely to all manner of vices and debauchery, among which the first is that of drunkenness, which they exercise for the most part with brandy. This they drink as liberally as the Spaniards do clear fountain water."

THE SACK OF CARTAGENA

The last great buccaneer raid was the sack of Cartagena in 1689. Sir Francis Drake had attacked Cartagena in the 1580s, but most buccaneers had avoided it since because of its strong defenses. The 1689 attack was organized by the French government with a fleet of ten French warships under the command of Baron Jean de Pointis, seven ships provided by buccaneers, and several more by Jean Du Casse, the French governor of Saint Dominique. Cartagena surrendered on May 6, 1689, whereupon Baron de Pointis agreed to take only half of the city's wealth; this enraged the buccaneers and Du Casse, who had received only a tiny part of their agreed booty from de Pointis. So after de Pointis left, the buccaneers sacked Cartagena again, this time with much brutality and torture. They returned to Saint Dominique with the remaining wealth of the city, but were ambushed by an English fleet and lost most of their plunder. When de Pointis arrived back in France, King Louis XIV sent the buccaneers a sum of money to show his gratitude. However, the whole operation had been a big disappointment for the buccaneers, and after that many of them turned to legal privateering or piracy against any nation.

THE GOLDEN AGE OF PIRACY

The end of the seventeenth century saw a huge surge in piracy, now known as the golden age of piracy even though it only lasted about forty years, from around 1690 to 1730. This era made living legends of Blackbeard and Bartholomew Roberts, who operated in the Caribbean and off the Atlantic coast of America, and Henry Avery, William Kidd, and Thomas Tew, who operated off the coast of West Africa and the Indian Ocean.

During the age of the buccaneers, which preceded the golden age, Spanish interests had been the main target. Now, anyone was fair game, especially the merchant ships which sailed from Europe to the American colonies, bringing slaves from Africa and returning with rum, cocoa, and sugar. The days of huge convoys of Spanish ships sailing with hoards of gold, silver, and jewels was over, but an even larger trade in commodities replaced it.

Many factors combined to create the golden age. Buccaneering was coming to an end, and as a result many buccaneers turned to piracy or privateering. The outbreak of war between England and France resulted in many privateering contracts. When the Treaty of Utrecht helped to end the Spanish War of Succession in 1713, there was mass unemployment as thousands of seamen were released from military service; many of them turned to piracy. Life for those seamen who were able to find legitimate employment on the European slave ships was wretched: they endured terrible working conditions, as job shortages forced down wages, and the mortality rate for slave ship crews exceeded thirty percent. For them, piracy became a far more attractive option.

Owing to a lack of strong central government, the American colonies were an easy target for pirates. Colonial governors initially welcomed pirate contraband, until they were in a stronger economic position and could begin to clamp down on piracy. By 1730, the golden age was over, but it is this period that has been immortalized and romanticized in the popular culture ever since, through books such as Captain Charles Johnson's *A General History of the Robberies and Murders of the Most Notorious Pyrates*, Robert Louis Stevenson's *Treasure Island*, and J. M. Barrie's *Peter Pan*.

MADAGASCAR

Pirates who operated off West Africa and in the Indian Ocean attacked Indian and Arab ships, the most prized of all being the East Indian trading ships (ships belonging to the British East India Company) which sailed from the East to the markets of Europe, laden with spices, silk, and porcelain. This trade route had been opened up after Portuguese navigator Vasco da Gama returned from India in the late fifteenth century. The Portuguese dominated these sea routes during the sixteenth century, but by the mid-seventeenth century the Dutch and English were major trading presences that had pushed the Portuguese into third place.

Madagascar is a large island located approximately 250 miles off the coast of East Africa. It was the stop-off point for ships before they rounded the Cape of Good Hope, and it was ideally placed for raids in the Indian Ocean. Being over a thousand miles long, its coast allowed numerous places for pirates to hide out, plus it had plentiful supplies of food. The native population was relatively small, and thus posed little threat to the pirates.

Madagascar became the prime base for piracy in the Indian Ocean during the golden age. Pirates took advantage of the internal warfare within the great Moghul Empire to seize control of the Indian Ocean for a period of about twenty years until the East India Company and others started sailing in huge convoys for increased protection.

Pirate bases at Madagascar were formed at Ranter Bay, St. Augustine Bay, and St. Mary's Island on the east coast (as well as Reunion Island

and Mauritius). In 1700, St. Mary's Island alone was home to 2,000 pirates and more than twenty ships. By 1711, the number of pirates living there had dwindled to less than a hundred after merchant ships were organized into convoys, and fleets of warships patrolled around the pirate bases. However, piracy in the Indian Ocean didn't end there. Coastal fiefdoms sprung up due to the lack of centralized government control in India, and pirates continued to operate from these areas during the first half of the eighteenth century, before the East India Company managed to wipe these out too.

PIRATES IN THE FAR EAST

Pirates have menaced the Far East since the sixth century A.D. After the Han dynasty ended in A.D. 220, Chinese politics became decentralized and piracy was allowed to spread in Chinese waters, as coastal warlords traded goods and attacked rival ships. Even when the Ming dynasty restored order to China in the fourteenth century, the sheer size of Chinese coastal waters made controlling piracy a difficult challenge, as rival clans fought each other for regional control of the sea.

It took the Ming dynasty a century to gain control, often by sending state funds to coastal warlords to suppress one another. The result was that provincial corruption was inadvertently supported by the state.

By the sixteenth century, the Ming dynasty was giving titles and salaries to pirates in an attempt to turn them into pirate hunters. By the seventeenth century the first Chinese pirate empire emerged, created by Cheng Chi Lung. Cheng's pirate fleet was so large (consisting of more than 1,000 junks) that in 1627 the Dutch governor of Batavia reported, "Commercial navigation has totally ceased." Eventually the emperor made him an admiral in the hope that he would turn pirate hunter. Instead, Cheng made a deal with the Manchu rulers in Beijing and helped to topple the Ming dynasty, after which the Manchu rulers had him executed because he was too powerful.

After Cheng's execution in 1661, his son Kuo Hsing Yeh sought revenge, and extended his father's pirate empire even further. He cut off the city of Nanking, prevented foreigners from using the Yangtze River, and regained the pirate province of Fukien that his father had handed over to the Manchus. By now, piracy in the Far East was so widespread that it became an extension of Chinese politics. When Kuo

Hsing Yeh died in 1683, he was regarded as a hero who had fought to preserve the Ming cultural dynasty from the Europeans as well as from the Manchus. Piracy aimed against European interlopers was considered patriotic, and so imperial ambivalence towards piracy continued.

During the eighteenth century, piracy spread into Vietnam and the Indonesian archipelago, and the pirate dynasty of Cheng I became the biggest pirate confederation in history—big enough to resist attacks from the emperor's forces. Cheng I controlled the Chinese coast from Korea to the Indo-Chinese Peninsula, with a confederation of over 150,000 pirates. His huge fleet was divided into six color-coded squadrons, each assigned its own territory. The flagship squadron took the color red and became known as the Red Fleet. It numbered 600 junks and more than 30,000 pirates. Cheng I even issued protection passes to paying ships which, for a fee, guaranteed safe passage from attack by any of his fleets.

After his death in 1807, Cheng I's wife, a Cantonese prostitute named Shih Yang (known as Cheng I Sao, or "Wife of Cheng"), took over command of the confederation. This was not unusual in Chinese culture, as the whole family lived on the junks and the women fought alongside the men. Cheng I Sao proved to be an outstanding leader *(see page 159)*, until jealousy from one of the fleet commanders over her choice of a new husband caused internal warfare that broke up the federation. Piracy in the Far East was eventually eradicated by European traders and the Opium Wars.

THE AGE OF PRIVATEERING

Privateering—legitimate piracy supported by a privateer's government—was first recorded in the seventeenth century. Men such as Sir Francis Drake were privateers, but the great age of privateering took place after France and Spain resumed war against each other in the 1740s. The main arena was the Caribbean, but privateers also operated in the greater Atlantic. Eighteenth-century trade was wide-ranging: sugar, molasses, cotton from colonial plantations, tools, weapons, and South American spices were shipped to Europe, and the slave trade still operated from Europe to the Americas.

The United States used privateers to oppose the British following the rebellion of American colonies in 1775. More than 3,000 British merchant ships were captured during this period, bringing a lucrative income stream to the American government. The War of 1812 between Britain and America saw the launching of several "super privateers" who attacked British shipping in the Atlantic and whose ships were large enough that they could sail to Europe and to the Pacific and Indian Oceans.

The last great wave of piracy took place after the end of the Napoleonic Wars in 1815. For about fifteen years, South American independence movements relied on privateers to attack Spanish shipping to break the Spanish colonial stranglehold. Even after peace was declared between Britain and the U.S., many Latin American privateers continued their struggle against Spain, and also plundered American vessels, long after European and U.S. privateering had ended. This pirate activity was smaller in scale, but brutal in its operation. Historian Angus Konstam explains that "many of the new pirates were small-time robbers . . . [who] frequently murdered their victims to prevent anyone identifying them later. While men like Bartholomew Roberts plundered wealthy cargoes and spared the crew during the golden age of piracy, in the 1820s sailors were often massacred for the clothes they wore."

During the 1820s, the U.S. and British navies worked hard to wipe out these pirates, and by the end of the decade the pirate threat was effectively curtailed. Large-scale piracy became a thing of the past, and lived on only in the legends, stories, and romantic myths that survive to this day.

Chapter 2

Life Aboard a Pirate Ship

To understand why men turned to piracy and how pirates lived, it is useful to examine what life was like for "ordinary" sailors. Life at sea was grim. Dr. Samuel Johnson said, "No man will be a sailor who had contrivance enough to get himself into jail; for being in a ship is being in a jail with the chance of being drowned."

OPPORTUNITIES ON SHORE

During the golden age of piracy (1690–1730) there were few employment options for men, women, and children of low birth. Most were illiterate and three-quarters of the population of England lived rurally and in extreme poverty. Rural life was just as hard as trying to make a living in the city. A few lucky young men became apprentices in a trade, but a large number turned to crime in order to eat or to stay out of debtors' prison.

The merchant navy at least offered the opportunity to learn a trade. A seaman could master all the tasks required on board, and then be hired onto another vessel for a higher wage. He might also learn trades such as cooperage or carpentry that he could use later on land. But many men signed up for a life of adventure on the high seas with little awareness of the horrors that awaited them.

Many young boys were attracted to the sea as an alternative to a life on the street, being a chimney sweep, or doing some other hard and dangerous form of child labor. Children as young as eight signed on as cabin boys. They would perform a range of duties from cleaning the deck to polishing the brass. Also, boys were used as "powder monkeys" to carry gunpowder from the hold to the gun decks. Within a few years, a boy would be performing all the duties of an adult sailor.

PRESS GANGS

The Royal Navy paid two months' wages in advance when a man signed up, which helped keep many recruits out of debtors' prison for debts of less than twenty pounds. The merchant navy, on the other hand, paid six months in arrears to deter crew from deserting. Despite this contrast, few city dwellers were tempted to join the navy voluntarily, so most sailors had to be "pressed" into service.

The admiralty created the "Impress Service," which operated at every English port. By law, the Impress Service could forcibly recruit any man between the ages of eighteen and fifty-five. It used gangs of tough wharf laborers to search the ports looking for victims. Many wharf laborers joined the press gangs to avoid being drafted.

Men living in ports soon learned to hide whenever they saw a man-of-war approaching the shore. As a result, the press gangs had to sail inland to find recruits, so that increasingly sailors came from rural communities.

Even merchant seamen could be seized by the Impress Service. Press gangs were allowed to board any ship and take their pick, so long as they left behind a skeleton crew.

Simple trickery was another effective way of gaining recruits. The expression "taking the king's shilling" referred to the practice of offering men twelve pennies (a shilling) to join up. If a man accepted, he was enlisted, even if he was tricked into it. It was common practice for the recruiters to drop a shilling into a man's pint in an alehouse or tavern. When the victim had nearly finished his drink, he would notice something at the bottom and fish it out. He would then be grabbed by a group of burly men from the press gang and informed that he had just accepted the king's shilling, and be carted off to sea. Tankards with glass bottoms became popular as a direct result of this practice, so that men could be sure there wasn't a shilling hiding at the bottom.

THE ROYAL NAVY

Once on board, a seaman's life was brutal. Life on a ship was dangerous and difficult for a Navy seaman and pirate alike, but a Navy man was a virtual prisoner. He would be away at sea for months on end, and when the ship docked he would rarely be allowed ashore, to prevent him from deserting. The discipline was harsh. The captain was God. If a sadistic captain took a dislike to certain members of his crew, he could work them to death, or have them brutally punished for the most minor infractions, such as an incorrect salute.

Flogging was the most common punishment. The captain decided the number of lashes, and this was formally set down in 1755. Usually the minimum was ten lashes; fifty would cause severe injury, and 100 was often fatal. The whip was the infamous cat-o'-nine-tails, a hemp or leather rope with nine lashes, with at least three "blood knots" tied to the end of each lash. This brutal weapon could easily strip the skin to the bone. For further torture, vinegar or salt was rubbed into the wound. In the Navy, the flogging cat was kept in a red bag tied to the mast, and all sailors dreaded "letting the cat out of the bag."

The average life expectancy for a sailor was between thirty and thirty-five years, compared to more than fifty years for those who remained on land. A sailor wore the clothes that he was wearing when he enlisted and usually slept in them as well. New clothes were too expensive for seamen earning their ordinary wage, so they wore the clothes on their back until they disintegrated into rags. A new set of clothes might set a sailor back two months' wages. By stark and cruel contrast, the officers, who were second sons from noble families, had their own chests of tailor-made clothes.

HOW TO BECOME A PIRATE

Pirates came from all nationalities and backgrounds, but during the golden age of piracy, most were Welsh. There were many Irish and English pirates and fewer Scots. French and Spanish pirateering was widespread. There were also a lot of runaway black slaves, known as "Cimarron" (Spanish for maroon), and there were several famous black pirates, such as Diego Grillo and Lauren de Graff.

Pirates recruited crews both on land and at sea. On land, a pirate captain would let it be known that his ship was "going on the account," and those interested in joining would sign on voluntarily. Their decision would be based on the reputation of the captain; if he was a man renowned for returning from his excursions with rich pickings, he would have no shortage of willing volunteers. Recruits had to bring their own weapons: at the very least a pistol, blackpowder and shot, and a sword. Men with additional weapons were in demand. Shipmates who were musicians, or who had skills such as carpentry and cooperage, were even more desirable, and were often seized by pirates and forced to join the crew.

At sea, men were recruited from seized ships. Whenever pirates took control of a ship, the common sailors were given the choice of joining. Any who did so immediately became marked men, but at least they escaped the harsh naval or merchant life for the promise of riches and greater personal freedom. However, many sailors made it appear as though they were being taken against their will, so that if they were caught by authorities at a later date they could plead innocence. They were made to sign "shipboard articles of conduct," a set of pirate rules. This document could also be presented at a subsequent trial to prove coercion.

Passengers were also vulnerable, and anyone with a professional skill was usually snatched. Often, the officers and passengers had to be whipped and tortured *(see page 66)* to divulge who amongst them had special skills.

Sometimes merchant vessels became pirate ships after a mutiny by the crew. For example, Henry Avery (also known as Every) was the first mate of the *Charles* when he organized a mutiny while the captain was sleeping off a night of heavy drinking. He renamed the ship *Fancy* and within months had become one of the most prolific and famous pirates in history.

THE PIRATE CREW

Sailing a ship required an experienced team of men. Apart from the ordinary pirate crew, there were several important posts upon which the crew's success and survival depended:

Captain

A few captains such as Blackbeard *(see page 137)* ruled their crew with the brutality and ruthlessness that was customary in the Navy, but on the whole the captain was elected by majority vote and only remained in command by his own merit. According to Johnson's *A General History of the Pyrates*, the only time the captain's position was secure was when "fighting, chasing or being chased." At any other time if he failed to secure food or plunder, or if he lost the faith of the majority of the crew, he could quickly find himself voted out of his position.

The captain's main perk was that he received the greatest share of the booty, but in other respects he was like everyone else. For example, the captain had the best sleeping quarters, but any member of the crew supposedly was allowed to enter his room, eat off his plate, and sleep in his bed.

The captains who consistently led pirate sorties and brought back happy, wealthy shipmates gained the reputation of being "pistol proof." This reputation would guarantee them a good supply of willing and skilled recruits.

Navigator

Known on board as "the artist," the navigator knew the strange art of setting the ship's course and plotting its whereabouts using maps; mathematics; and (to the rest of the crew) mysterious instruments, such as the compass, the "bring-'em-near" (telescope), and the astro-labe (to calculate the altitude of the sun and stars).

Good navigators were a rarity and a navigator's sea charts were his most prized possession. A skilled navigator could bring a ship within a few miles upwind of its destination, so that it could drift downwind into port. Arriving off the coast a few miles downwind could be a disaster. In 1720 Bartholomew Roberts was a few miles off the coast of West Africa but couldn't beat prevailing trade winds to reach his destination, so he had to turn around and sail across the Atlantic back to South America before making a second attempt.

Quartermaster

Elected by the crew, the quartermaster was technically the second-in-command, but he supervised the daily running of the ship. Because it was his job to settle disputes and to make sure that the captain's orders were carried out, he had to be one of the toughest men on the ship. He was also the trial judge responsible for meting out punishment for minor offenses. If a serious offense was committed, the crew and captain acted as jury with the quartermaster as judge. He was also usually the only crewmember who could administer a flogging, following the majority vote of the crew.

The quartermaster led the boarding party when raiding a captured ship and took charge of dividing up the plunder after a raid, ensuring that each man received what had been set down in the articles of conduct—a skill that nevertheless required a mixture of diplomacy and unchallenged authority.

Carpenter/Surgeon

A surgeon was a rare catch on any ship, and in practice it was usually the ship's carpenter who performed this duty, because he was the one with the tools of the trade, namely a saw for performing amputations. The boatswain was on hand with a red-hot ax to cauterize the wounds, and the sail-maker would do the suturing.

The carpenter was responsible for keeping the ship's hull and mast sound. In the heat of battle, he and his team would shore up leaks and patch holes. After an enemy ship had been captured, the carpenter performed a speedy inspection before deciding whether the prize was seaworthy.

Cooper

Since food and drink and many other supplies such as lamp oil and gunpowder were stowed in wooden barrels, the skill of the barrel-maker was vital to the well being of the crew. His vigilance ensured that the barrels were kept as air- or water-tight as possible. To save space, barrels were assembled and dismantled as required.

Boatswain

The daily maintenance and inventory of ship's supplies, from tar and tallow to sails and tackle, was managed by the boatswain. He was the most experienced sailor on board, and his expert knowledge of the rigging and sails meant the difference between life and death.

Master gunner

The master gunner maintained the ship's cannons and ensured that the gunpowder was kept safe and dry. He trained the teams of men who operated the cannons and kept them battle-ready.

Cook

This position was often taken by a member of the crew who had gained a severe battle injury that prevented him from performing other more demanding duties. Preparing palatable meals when the ship's food quickly became rotten within a few weeks into a voyage was a tough challenge.

Musicians

Anyone who could play an instrument was a valuable member of the crew. Musical entertainment was important to boost morale and to relieve boredom. Jigs and nautical shanties were well-liked and loud martial music was played during battle.

LIVING CONDITIONS

A pirate ship was a much dirtier place to live than a Navy vessel. The deck was rarely washed, and conditions below decks were even worse.

Space was a premium, so the toughest pirates would fight to sleep in one of the hammocks that were strung out below deck, less than a foot and a half apart. When space ran out there, the rest of the crew had to sleep in the open, but nowhere on the ship came anything close to "comfortable." Below deck the combined smell of unwashed bodies, "piss tubs" kept in the corridors to put out fires, fetid food, and putrid bilge water was atrocious. Dampness permeated everything, so pirates lived with constant dankness: clothes were difficult to get dry, and nobody ever washed.

These were ideal breeding conditions for the many diseases that could quickly strike down a whole crew. Injuries and wounds quickly became infected and gangrenous, and in warm climates mosquitoes spread malaria, cholera, yellow fever, and typhus. Poor diet and hygiene caused scurvy, dysentery, and diarrhea. There could scarcely have been a time on board when there weren't several members of the crew with no control of their bodily functions. On top of this, sexually transmitted diseases were rampant. The ship's surgeon spent more time treating the myriad infections than tending to battle wounds.

While many a pirate was killed by disease, the daily hazards involved in running a ship claimed significant lives. Falling was a common way to suffer injury or death. Climbing up and down the ratlines (rope ladders) on the mast and rigging was dangerous in calm dry weather; during a storm, with high winds, huge swells, and waves crashing all

around, even the most experienced sailor could lose his footing and fall to his death.

In the Caribbean during the hurricane season (summer to early fall), storms regularly appeared without warning, and any ship that had not reached a safe port would have no alternative but to ride it out. If the mast snapped, the ship was dead in the water. Sometimes the captain had to make the tough decision to cut the mast to take the pressure off the hull, because if the ship snapped in half, the entire crew was sent to "Davy Jones's Locker." Crews would work the pumps and use buckets to bale out the water for hours on end. If the storm was really fierce, the crew would be forced to throw heavy items such as cannons and provisions overboard, and cut away the anchors to lighten their vessel. So, even if a pirate ship survived a storm, the crew faced a grim future with no provisions and diminished firepower.

Even worse than high winds was no wind at all. When a ship was becalmed in the middle of the ocean, the crew would be faced with weeks of mind-numbing boredom, waiting for a breeze, while watching the food and water run out. Many a pirate crew suffered a slow and agonizing death on motionless ships.

FOOD AND DRINK

When a pirate ship set sail, food—barrels of salted fish and other meats, cheese, hard tack (biscuits)—and water would be fresh and abundant. Within weeks it would be rotten. The cheese became so hard the men would carve their rations to make buttons and other items. The damp conditions below deck were a breeding ground for insects and parasites: black-headed maggots and weevils infested all the food. Men often preferred to eat in the dark so they couldn't see what they were putting in their mouths.

Before eating hard tack it was banged on the table to make the maggots wriggle out. If the maggot was gray and plump the biscuit was still edible; if the maggot was pallid and thin, there was no goodness left in it.

Spirits such as rum, wine, brandy, sherry, and beer were always drunk in preference to water. Rum was the most popular drink. It was drunk hot or cold and flavored with spices. It was made from molasses and didn't go sour like beer or wine.

Other pirate beverages included *bombo*, a blend of rum, water, sugar, and nutmeg; *rumbullion*, made from rum, wine, tea, lime juice, sugar, and spices; and *rumfustian*, a mixture of raw eggs, sherry, gin, and beer.

Whenever a ship was captured, seizing fresh food was a priority, along with all the spices that could disguise the taste of rancid provisions. Any alcohol on board was quickly drunk, and the rest was used to clean the deck. It was not uncommon for a pirate crew to be caught unawares because they were too drunk to put up a fight.

If food ran short, the men hunted for sea turtles, which could be kept alive and fresh by flipping them on their backs. Francis Rogers, on a visit to Jamaica in 1704, described this delicacy: "The flesh looks and eats much like choice veal, but the fat is of a green color, very luscious

and sweet; the liver is likewise green, very wholesome, searching
and purging."

Pirates didn't fish off the side of the ship, because shoals of fish avoided
large moving objects, but they frequently shot birds and when on land
would hunt cattle, goats, and pigs. When things became really desperate, the men resorted to eating bugs and the ship's rats.

A common pirate meal was *salmagundi*, a heavily spiced stew that
contained whatever ingredients were available, including turtle, fish,
meat, cabbage, wine, garlic, pickled onions, oil, eggs, grapes, and
olives. In more exotic climes, even monkeys, snakes, and oysters
would be thrown into the pot.

George Roberts, who spent time as a captive on Edward Low's ship,
gives a vivid description of meal times in his 1726 book *The Four Years
Voyages of Capt. George Roberts.* He observed with much distaste that
the crew ate dinner "in a very disorderly manner more like a kennel of
hounds, than like men, snatching and catching the victuals from one
another; which, though it was odious to me, it seemed one their chief
diversions, and, the said, looked martial-like."

Another captive, Philip Ashton, described pirate behavior after his experience in 1722: "I soon found that any death was preferable to being
linked with such a vile crew of miscreants, to whom it was a sport to
do mischief, where prodigious drinking, monstrous cursing and swearing, hideous blasphemies . . . was the constant employment, unless
when sleep something abated the noise and revellings."

Drunkenness was the natural state for most pirates. If there was no work to do, the men would be incapacitated by drink. At their trials many pirates attempted to mitigate their crimes by blaming alcohol. In 1724 pirate John Archer blamed his criminality on "brutish drunkenness. By strong drink I have been heated and hardened into the crimes that are now more bitter than death to me."

THE PIRATE CODE OF CONDUCT

The social system aboard a pirate ship was egalitarian and there truly was honor amongst thieves. This was a direct reaction against the authoritarianism many pirates would have experienced as sailors on board a merchant vessel. As historian Paul Gilbert points out: "Nearly 100 years before the American and French Revolutions, experiments in egalitarian democracy were being carried out on the decks of hundreds of pirate ships."

Justice and fairness were the watchwords of the pirate life. Each man received his fair share of booty and all men were equals.

In return for his freedom, pirates were bound by articles of conduct, which if they were broken resulted in severe punishment or sometimes death. The eleven articles used by Black Bart Roberts, as reported in Angus Konstam's *The History of Pirates*, are a typical example of the pirate code:

1. Every man shall have an equal vote in affairs of the moment. He shall have an equal title to the fresh provisions or strong liquors at any time seized, and shall use them at pleasure unless a scarcity may make it necessary for the common good that a retrenchment may be voted.

2. Every man shall be called fairly to turn by the list on board of prizes. But if they defraud the company to the value of even one dollar in plate, jewels, or money, they shall be marooned. If any man rob another he shall have his nose and ears slit, and be put ashore where he shall be sure to encounter hardships.

3. None shall game for money either with dice or cards.

4. The lights and candles shall be put out at eight at night, and if any of the crew desire to drink after that hour they shall sit upon the deck without lights.

5. Each man shall keep his piece, cutlass, and pistols at all times clean and ready for action.

6. No boy or woman to be allowed amongst them. If any man shall be found seducing any of the latter sex and carrying her to sea in disguise, he shall suffer death.

7. He that shall desert the ship or his quarters in time of battle shall be punished by death or marooning.

8. None shall strike another on board the ship, but every man's quarrel shall be ended on shore by sword or pistol in [a duel].

9. No man shall talk of breaking up their way of living till each has a share of £1,000. Every man who shall become a cripple or lose a limb in the service shall have eight hundred pieces-of-eight from the common stock and for lesser hurts proportionately.

10. The captain and the quartermaster shall each receive two shares of a prize, the master gunner and bosun one and one half shares, all other officers one and one quarter, and private gentlemen of fortune one share each.

11. The musicians shall have rest by right on the Sabbath Day only. On all other days by favor only.

If a pirate suffered a crippling injury he received compensation from the rest of the crew, on a sliding scale depending on the severity of the damage. Exquemelin, in *Buccaneers of America*, records that the loss of a right arm brought the highest compensation at 600 pieces-of-eight; the left arm or right leg were each worth 500 pieces; the left leg was worth 400; and an eye 100 pieces.

PIRATE PUNISHMENT AND TORTURE

Pirate punishments for misdeeds were many and varied. There are also reports of the many ways in which pirates tortured their captives.

A common punishment for murder was to tie the murderer to the corpse and toss them overboard.

Keelhauling involved tying the offender to the main yard and attaching weights to his feet. An oil-soaked rag was stuffed into his mouth to keep him from drowning, and then he was dragged under the hull and up the other side. In the process he would have the skin stripped from his back by the barnacles on the hull. The process was repeated three times and was often fatal.

Marooning was a less cruel but no more desirable punishment. Being put ashore on a deserted island far away from normal trade routes was a virtual death sentence.

Sweating a man to death involved having him run up and down the deck or rigging until he collapsed or fell to his death. The pirate Francis Farrington Spriggs was known to sweat his captives by having them run around the decks while the crew pricked them with knives and other sharp objects.

The hated Navy practice of flogging was only used on a pirate ship in the severest of cases.

Walking the plank has become synonymous with pirate punishment of captives, but in fact it was very rare, and the only pirate who made his victims walk the plank was Major Stede Bonnet. Pirates did, however, feed their victims to sharks. Furthermore, so few sailors could swim that simply being tossed overboard could be fatal. The plank-walking legend seems to have originated with a mutineer seaman named George Wood who, shortly before being hung in Newgate Prison in 1769, claimed that he and others had made loyal crewmen walk the plank. This idea was later popularized by the nineteenth century author and illustrator Howard Pyle.

PASSING THE TIME

There were three times as many men on board as was needed to sail the ship; this was to replace men lost due to sickness or injury. This meant that there was a lot of free time, especially when there was no wind and the ship sat becalmed for days on end.

Drinking was the favorite leisure activity, and it was often accompanied by the singing of rowdy shanties and dancing. Staging mock trials was another way pirates passed the time. Capture and execution for piracy was a constant threat, so role-playing was a reasonable means of making light of the menace. The crew members were assigned roles of lawyer, judge, jailer, and hangman, and the game was played out with a level of realism that was sometimes hard to distinguish from the real thing. On one occasion, in 1717, a mock trial was so realistic that the man in the dock became so afraid he threw a grenade at the "judge," then drew his cutlass and sliced off the prosecutor's arm.

During quieter moments, pirates passed the time as regular sailors might: they carved wood, bone, and pieces of hard cheese, or created intricate knot-work decorations around personal possessions.

Card or dice games were very popular. Dice were made out of cheese or musket shot and boards were made from old bits of canvas.

Chapter 3

Attack!
Battle Tactics and Weapons

The pirate's greatest weapon was fear. Some pirates, such as Blackbeard *(see page 137)*, were so feared that if they raised their flag to identify themselves, their hapless enemies would often surrender rather than fight. Bartholomew "Black Bart" Roberts once sailed into Newfoundland's Bay of Trespassey where he plundered and scuppered twenty-two vessels without meeting any resistance. The crews had seen him coming and they fled.

Some pirates, including Blackbeard and Edward Low, were sadistic and enjoyed torturing captives for sport. For most pirates, however, torture and violence were merely tools for maintaining a fearsome reputation. Pirates who were feared met less resistance and didn't have to engage in as many battles, which cost men, ships, and ammunition. However, many had already spent brutal years as seamen before they became pirates, so the treatment that they had received on board a merchant ship would have turned many into brutalized and irremediably violent killers. As David Cordingly points out in *Life Among the Pirates*, "the real world of the pirates was often closer to some of today's horror movies than anything which appeared in contemporary books or plays."

Many stories of pirates have romanticized and sanitized their exploits. For example, John Gow, alias John Smith, was thirty-five when he led a mutiny on board the *George Galley* on November 3, 1724, then headed for the Orkney Islands. He abducted three women from the island of Cava. According to Daniel Defoe, the women were "kept on board some time, and used so inhumanly, that when they set them on shore again, they were not able to go or to stand; and we hear that one of them died on the beach where they left them." Despite this horrific behavior, a century later Sir Walter Scott used Gow's story for his historical novel *The Pirate*, but played down his atrocities.

Cordingly cites the depositions of two seamen about treatment meted out by Charles Vane as examples of the violence common among pirates. The first was Nathaniel Catling, who was aboard the Bermuda sloop *Diamond* in April 1718 when it was attacked by Vane aboard the *Ranger*. The captain and crew were violently assaulted and Vane's men kidnapped a black man and stole 300 pieces-of-eight. Catling was hung until seemingly dead, but when he revived later, one of the crew slashed him across his collarbone with his cutlass. They then burned the *Diamond*. The second account is from Edward North of the Bermuda sloop *William and Martha*, who witnessed one of his crew being tied to the bowsprit and then having his eyes burned out with matches, while a pistol muzzle was stuffed in his mouth, "thereby to oblige him to confess what money was on board."

While the treatment of these men was excessive, the motive was clear—to terrify and to quickly get captives to divulge the whereabouts of valuables. Cordingly gives a third reason for violence: "Pirates were quick to avenge any attempt to curb their activities, and many atrocities were revenge attacks on islands or the ships of nations which had imprisoned or hanged pirates in the recent past."

Edward Low reveled in the suffering of others. His sadism was notorious in the Caribbean. In March of 1724, Governor Hart described how Low captured a Portuguese ship returning to Brazil. After the captain threw a huge sack of gold into the sea, Low "cut off the said Master's lips and broiled them before his face, and afterwards murdered the whole crew being thirty-two persons."

Even Henry Morgan, who claimed that he treated prisoners well, is reported to have cruelly tortured captives from Porto Bello in Spain. He burned the private parts of female prisoners and roasted another woman on a baking stove because they would not tell Morgan where they had hidden their money.

The methods which pirates used to torture their victims were as inventive as they were varied. A popular method involved tying cords around the victim's limbs, stretching them, and beating them with sticks and swords. Pressing people to death by laying heavy stones on their chests was also widespread.

Exquemelin describes a pirate torture of prisoners called "woolding" in which "slender cords or matches twisted about their heads, till their eyes burst out of the skull." One particularly gruesome torture was devised by Montbars of Languedoc. He nailed one end of a person's lower intestines to the mast then made them dance a jig around it so that the rest of their bowel unwound, while they were beaten with burning sticks.

WEAPONRY

Pirates had a range of technology at their disposal to take on the might of Navy vessels and merchants ships.

Cannons

Cannons were labor-intensive weapons that required teams of four or more men to operate—one man to load, and another three to aim, fire, and reposition. Operating the cannon was a specialized skill and required a lot of practice. A well-trained team could fire a round every few minutes.

During the eighteenth century, a cannon had an effective range of up to 2,000 yards and the largest cannons could fire balls that weighed thirty-two pounds. The weight of the cannon dramatically increased in relation to the weight of the shot, although the ratio between powder and shot decreased with increased shot size. The master gunner had to have expert knowledge for the cannons to hit their targets without exploding. This diagram shows the relationship between cannon size, bore-size, ball weight, and powder required.

Ball weight	Bore size	Cannon weight	Gunpowder
2 pounder	2.5 inches	600 lb	3.5 lb
4 pounder	3 inches	1,000-1500 lb	6 lb
24 pounder	4.5 inches	3,000-4,000 lb	14 lb
32 pounder	5 inches	4,000-5,000 lb	18 lb

The popular myth is that pirates loaded their ships with lots of cannons, but in fact many pirates preferred to sacrifice firepower for lightness and speed. So long as a pirate ship could get close enough for

its crew to use muskets, grenades, sangrenels, blunderbusses, and grappling hooks, the pirates could overrun the enemy ship because pirate crews usually outnumbered their quarry's crews several times over. Some pirate ships carried only two cannons, one on each side of the ship. Outrunning a ship and capturing it without damage was always preferable to a prolonged artillery battle. Often, a warning shot across the bow was enough to frighten the crew into surrendering. If that failed, a few rounds of chain or bar shot would make mincemeat of the rigging and sails.

If heavy artillery was used, there would be lots of splintered wood flying around on both ships, as masts, yards, and pieces of deck shattered after being hit by cannon shot. A large wooden splinter more than six inches long was called a "shiver." Many deaths resulted from shiver injuries and the infections that set in afterwards, and the term "shiver me timbers" is rooted in this common battle hazard.

During battle, ships maneuvered so that they could present their broadside to the enemy and fire a volley of guns simultaneously.

Operating the guns

When the captain or master gunner gave the order "clear for quarters," the crew would clear the area around the gun so that they could be made ready for action. Usually this meant clearing away hammocks, which were hung between the guns, as sleeping space was limited.

Sand was scattered on the deck to soak up water and blood and to keep the crew from slipping.

Several types of shot were used; the aim was to disable the ship rather than to destroy it:

✖ **Round shot:** this is the standard iron cannonball, however, it was not very accurate at long distances, so it was more popular as a medium-range projectile.

✖ **Bomb:** hollow iron balls were filled with powder and carried a fuse that was lit before they were fired. The aim was for the balls to explode on impact.

✖ **Bar shot:** big iron bars were devastating when they hit their target, but they were notoriously erratic in their trajectory.

✖ **Chain shot:** two iron balls joined together with a chain or small bar were designed to decimate rigging and sails, or wrap around the mast. They did little damage to decks or hulls but made a good medium-range weapon.

✖ **Bundle shot:** several short iron bars bundled together with rope could be fit neatly into the gun in a bundle. Once fired, they would spread apart and ricochet upon impact, splintering wood and bone, and ripping apart flesh. Bundle shot was a good anti-personnel weapon at short distances.

✖ **Grapeshot:** small iron balls wrapped in canvas or burlap were used as grapeshot, which would spread out over a wide area when fired from a gun.

✖ **Canister shot:** a large metal container could be filled with shot, glass, gravel, nails, and other deadly shrapnel (including coins, once the other ammunition ran out). Since it was more effective at close quarters, canister shot began to replace grapeshot during the 1800s.

HAND-THROWN PROJECTILES

Sangrenel

This anti-personnel round consisted of a cloth bag filled with small jagged scraps of iron. It caused devastating injuries, and the shrapnel was almost impossible to remove without causing further damage.

Stinkpot

These were small clay pots filled with burning sulfur and thrown onto the deck from close range. This crude form of tear gas overwhelmed and disoriented the enemy just before the grappling hooks were thrown.

A more sophisticated variation on the stinkpot was a glass-handled jug that was filled with putrid meat, saltpeter, limestone, and a nauseating resin called asafetida. It could be outfitted with a fuse.

Hand grenade

Named for the Spanish word for the pomegranate (*granada*), which they resembled, these small glass bottles or clay pots were filled with gunpowder, broken glass, and scraps of iron. Their fuses were lit before they were thrown. They were also known as powder flasks.

Caltrop

The caltrop is an ancient weapon that the Romans called *tribulus* or *murex ferreus* (jagged iron). It is a cast-iron projectile with four spikes arranged so that it always lands with one of the spikes pointing in the air, while the other three form a stable base. The caltrop was very popular with French corsairs. Pirates walked around the deck in bare feet, so caltrop injuries were common.

Grappling hook

Also called grappling irons or grapnels, these mini-anchors were attached to a rope and could be thrown a long distance, enabling pirates to grab hold of a ship and then haul it closer for boarding. The throw didn't have to be particularly accurate, since the sharp spikes could catch on rigging, sail, or yardarm, as well as the sides of the ship.

GUNS

Swivel gun

This portable weapon was like a mini-cannon that could be carried to any part of the ship and used to blast small rounds at close range. It was very useful for repelling boarders.

Musket

This was the first reasonably accurate small arm, and it was the forerunner to the rifle. Some muskets even used a rifled barrel to improve accuracy. Early muskets used a matchlock firing mechanism, but these were later replaced by the flintlock, which was more reliable, especially in wet conditions.

The flintlock musket weighed between twelve and eighteen pounds and was about five feet long. Pirates mainly used it for long-range sniping; they favored the musketoon and blunderbuss for shooting at closer range. Muskets were muzzle-loaded. The powder, charge, and shot were loaded separately, and then tamped down. Before a battle, pirates would make up a dozen charges called "apostles," worn in a bandolier across the body and containing just the right amount of black powder to fire the shot.

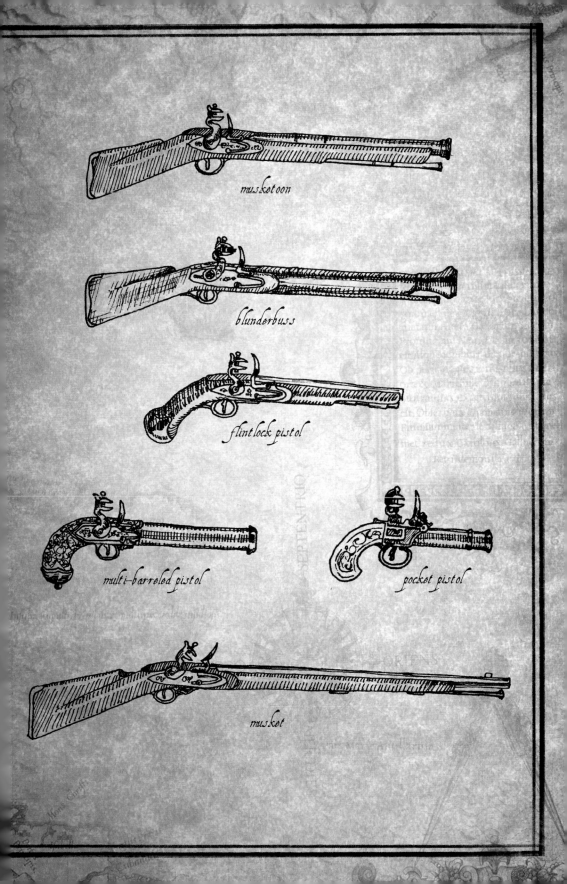

musketoon

blunderbuss

flintlock pistol

multi-barreled pistol

pocket pistol

musket

When fired in organized volleys muskets provided devastating fire-power every bit as effective as cannon shot. They were essential weapons for repelling boarders, but would be discarded at close quarters for pistols, which could be fired with one hand.

Blunderbuss

The sawed-off shotgun of its era, this muzzle-loading close-range weapon could fire a large ball, or cluster of pistol balls, nails, glass, or whatever other shrapnel was at hand. A blunderbuss could maim and kill several people with a single shot. It weighed between ten and sixteen pounds and was three feet long. The barrel bore was large—about two inches in diameter—and the end flared out like a funnel, which gave the weapon its wide shot pattern. The gun was usually fired from the hip, since it had a powerful recoil.

The blunderbuss was in use from as early as 1530 until the mid-nineteenth century. Its main drawback was that it was difficult to fire and slow to reload.

Musketoon

This was similar in operation and function to the blunderbuss, but was much shorter, making it less accurate than the musket, but easier to use in cramped close-combat conditions. It weighed between ten to fifteen pounds and was often shot from the shoulder.

Flintlock pistol

This comparatively lightweight and highly portable weapon was an ideal choice for personal defense, and the classic pistol of the golden age of piracy. Blackbeard carried six of them, holstered across his huge hairy chest. They weighed up to four or five pounds and were up to eighteen inches long.

"Flintlock" pistols were named for the firing mechanism, which superseded the earlier matchlock, wheel-lock, and snaphaunce firing mechanisms. When the trigger was pulled, a flint on the lock sent sparks into a priming pan that contained a small amount of black powder. This powder ignited the main charge inside the barrel. If the priming powder ignited, but the main charge failed, it was known as a "flash in the pan."

The lock-cock had to be pushed back two notches before the flintlock was ready to fire. When it was pushed back one notch, the gun was in the safety position known as "half-cocked." However, if it was handled roughly it could still "go off half-cocked." The term came to mean either that a person was exploding when they shouldn't, or that they weren't properly prepared.

The charges were prepared in advance, wrapped in paper waddings, and kept in a cartridge pouch worn at the hip. To load the flintlock, the end of the cartridge would be ripped open with the teeth; the contents were poured into the muzzle, followed by wadding and shot. Everything was tamped down with a small ramrod that was usually attached to the pistol to prevent it from getting lost.

Flintlocks were time-consuming to reload. As with most pirate firearms, they would be fired once and then either used as a club (the pistol grip had a metal cap on the end to act as a counterbalance), or holstered as combat switched to cutlass and knives.

Multi-barreled pistol

This muzzle-loaded pistol had two to four revolving barrels that fired separately using a single dog-head (hammer). The multi-fire capability was offset by its bulkiness and weight. These "turnover" pistols were difficult and expensive to produce, so they were rarer than other pistols. Rich gentlemen often carried gold or silver ones decorated with ivory as a conspicuous accessory; hence they made a fine prize for the discerning pirate.

Pocket pistol

A variety of tiny muzzle-loaded guns could be carried easily and concealed, so they were popular among the gentlemen and ladies of Europe for emergency close-range shooting. They usually fired a single shot, and were the forerunner of the derringer. These pistols were box-locked, which means that the dog-head was fitted centrally rather than to one side, making it easier to carry. However, this prevented the shooter from aiming straight down the barrel, making the pocket pistol accurate only at close range.

STABBING AND CUTTING WEAPONS

Cutlass

The cutlass was a cheap and unsophisticated weapon, but it was the sword of choice at sea. It was rough and heavy, with a broad curved blade that was usually about two feet long. The short blade was an advantage when fighting at close quarters; longer blades were more likely to get caught up in rigging and other obstacles on deck. When a deck was thronged with fighting men, there was rarely enough room to swing the type of long sword that officers in the Royal Navy used. The cutlass was used like a saber—it was a slashing, not a stabbing, weapon. Its size meant that a hacking cut could be performed quicker than the thrust of a rapier. Its thickness also made it easy to snap the blade of any opponent who wasn't using a cutlass.

The cutlass also had its uses outside of fighting. It was used for butchering meat (the cutlass is thought to have originated from the swords that were used by the early buccaneers for this purpose), cutting rope, or even cutting down trees.

Dusägge

This highly sought-after German cutlass was one of the most lethal bladed weapons in the pirate's arsenal during the late sixteenth and early seventeenth centuries. It had a serrated cutting edge that extended to the front section of the back of the blade. The hand protector, fashioned into a scallop shell, was both practical and decorative; the ridges in the metal allowed blood to flow away from the hand so that the handle remained dry and graspable.

Knives

There was a wide range of knives on board a pirate ship, including:

✘ **Dirk:** a small throwing knife with a long, thin, straight blade. Its origins date back to the Bronze Age when it was a short sword. *Dirk* is a Scottish word, probably derived from the Gaelic *sgian dearg* (red knife). Naval dirks were single- or double-edged; both were popular.

✘ **Main gauche:** a dagger that was used with a rapier in sixteenth- and seventeenth-century Europe. It was a sturdy double-edged weapon with a thick crossbar, used in the left hand (hence the name *gauche*, meaning left in French) to parry and block an opponent's weapon. A large triangular knuckle guard protected the hand, and on some versions two extra blades stuck out at an angle from the main blade to trap and break an opponent's sword.

✘ **Stiletto:** a European thrusting dagger that originated in Italy. Its blade was long (up to twenty inches) and narrow and without a cutting edge. The stiletto was often forged from a single piece of metal. It was a lethal stabbing weapon capable of inflicting deep puncture wounds.

✘ **Poignard:** a lightweight slender dagger with an exceptionally sharp tip.

✘ **Gully:** this was simply a big knife. All seamen carried one to cut food and perform on board duties such as cutting ropes. In the Navy, where only the officers were allowed other weapons, the commonplace gully was often instrumental during a mutiny. Some gullys folded like a penknife, and they did not have a hilt, like a dagger, so they couldn't be used to parry. They usually had one sharpened edge, and resembled modern kitchen knives.

✖ **Boucan knife:** the early Caribbean buccaneers used short, curved hacking weapons to cut up the wild animals that they hunted, such as wild boar and oxen. They looked like cut down cutlasses, and although they were utilitarian working knives, they were reasonably effective hacking weapons.

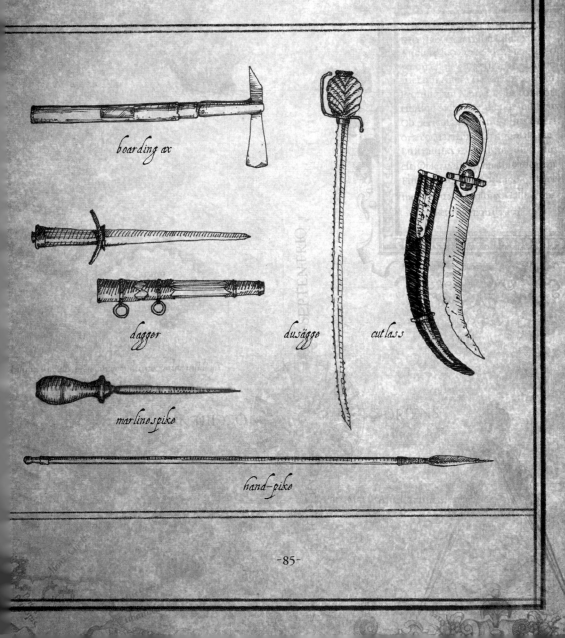

boarding ax

dagger

dusägge

cutlass

marlinespike

hand-pike

Boarding ax

This long-handled ax had a three-foot-long wooden handle and a two-pound iron head. It was sharpened on one side and flat on the other, so it could double as a sledgehammer. It was used to climb up the sides of a ship and cut rigging lines. When repelling an attack, the boarding ax was the best tool for cutting the rope away from any grappling hooks that landed on the ship. It was also used to smash down locked doors and hatches, or destroy locks. If the ship was fired on with hot cannon balls designed to lodge in the timbers and set fire to the ship, the boarding ax could chisel them out.

Marlinespike

Primarily a tool that doubled as a weapon, the marlinespike had a round blade with a sharp point set in a wooden handle. It was used to separate strands in marlines (a light rope made of two loosely twisted strands tarred together). Today, marlinespike seamanship refers to the art of handling and working with all kinds of natural fiber and wire rope, including knot-tying and splicing. Like the gully knife, the marlinespike was an essential piece of seafaring kit, which could not be locked away with the weapons, making it a lethal stabbing weapon during a mutiny.

Hand-pike

Also known as a halberd, the hand-pike was a metal-pointed spear with a long wooden shaft up to twenty feet long. It was used as a boarding weapon, and because of its length it was effective against swords and knives. It could also be thrown from great distances. Once an enemy ship had been boarded, the hand-pike was cast aside in favor of weapons more suited to close combat, such as the pistol or cutlass. Hand-pikes were used on ships in the New World and Caribbean long after they were replaced by the bayonet in land warfare.

Tomahawk

Named for the Algonquin words *tamahak* or *tamahakan,* the throwing hatchet was a Native American weapon that was later adopted by colonists and pirates. It could also be used as a parrying weapon and was effective during close-quarter combat.

The History of Paul Jones the Pirate, published in 1820, singles out this fearsome weapon: "The diversity of arms with which the party were equipped, farther confirmed the ill opinion entertained of the marauders; these consisted of muskets, pistols, swords, &c., and one fellow bore an American tomahawk over his shoulder."

Chapter 4

Pirate Ships, Flags, and Clothes

Ships, flags, and attire were all ways that pirates could broadcast their preeminence to the rest of the world. A fast ship, infamous flag, or the sight of a man such as Blackbeard with his fiery aspect could make the enemy surrender without a fight. In a business where plundering wealth depended upon instilling fear into one's victims, these three factors both contributed to and reflected a pirate's success.

PIRATE SHIPS

Pirates rarely built their own ships. Usually, they stole a ship and then customized it to their own needs. A pirate ship needed to be seaworthy, fast, maneuverable, and well-armed. When taking over a ship, the main considerations were seaworthiness and speed, because more weapons could always be added later. Daniel Defoe described a pirate ship as "a light pair of heels being of great use either to take, or to escape being taken." On a merchant vessel, the bulkheads, deck cabins, and one of the masts would often be removed, the quarter-deck lowered, and additional gun ports cut by the carpenter.

Most pirate ships could easily outsail other vessels on the sea, which was essential for both capturing ships and evading capture by the authorities. For example, when Charles Vane attacked ships in the Bahamas in 1718 he was able to outsail the authorities by "two foot for their one."

Most pirates kept one ship throughout their whole career (which was often brief—a matter of months rather than years; even Blackbeard's reign of terror lasted only a few years). Although some pirates changed ships—Bartholomew Roberts had six vessels in succession—a captured ship was usually sold or burned.

MAINTENANCE AND REPAIRS

Ships required regular maintenance, including repairs and careening (turning the boat over and cleaning the barnacles and weeds off the hull to keep it smooth). Ships were careened about once every three months. Pirates would sail into a safe haven and mount their cannons at the mouth of the bay to fight off a possible attack while the ship was being cleaned. The ship would then be beached and careened. The biggest threat to the structure of the hull was boring mollusks, such as the common teredo worm (also known as a shipworm), which burrowed into the wood and could grow up to six feet long. An infestation of these worms could destroy a hull during a long voyage.

Size matters

The size of the pirate ship was important. Large ships could ride out storms better than small ships could and carry more guns, but they were less maneuverable and harder to clean. Movies usually show pirates sailing large ships such as galleons, because they look so impressive, but in fact pirates favored small ships such as sloops, because they were fast and easier to maintain. Also, a small ship could sail into shallow water or hide among sandbanks to evade capture from a larger vessel.

Pirate crews were large so that sailing duties could be shared, but during combat teams of four to six men were needed to operate each cannon. A vessel with twelve cannons could need seventy men just to fire them, and require several powder monkeys as well.

The largest pirate ship to sail the Spanish Main was Blackbeard's
Queen Anne's Revenge; the only pirates with anything comparable
in size and force were Bartholomew Roberts *(see page 149)*, William
Moody, and Henry Avery.

MASTS AND RIGGING

Ships were classified according to their number of masts, their sail plan (the way the sails were rigged), and their number of gun decks. The mainmast is the middle mast on a three-masted ship, or the front mast on a two-masted ship. The mizzenmast is the rear mast, and the foremast the front mast on a three-masted ship.

The sails were rigged in two basic ways: square-rigged or fore-and-aft rigged. Square-rigging involves hanging the sails from yardarms—long pieces of timber, tapering towards the ends, hung by the center horizontally across and at right angles to (athwart) the mast. This sail plan catches a lot of wind from behind, but makes it hard to sail upwind. Typically, each mast would be divided into thirds, with three yard-arms and sails on each mast section: the topgallant mast, topmast, and lower mast. During a storm, square-rigged ships would switch to fore-and-aft rigging using special sails called trysails. These sails were attached to the lower mast to make the ship more stable and reduce the risk of capsizing.

Fore-and-aft rigging involves flying the sails from spars attached to the mainmast. Some ships also had triangular lateen sails that allow the ship to sail in a direction other than the wind direction. Fore-and-aft rigging catches less wind overall than square-rigging, but the sails can be moved to catch the wind, making the ship more maneuverable.

Many ships used a combination of rigging. A vessel with square-rigging on all three masts was "ship-rigged," whereas a ship with square-rigging on the fore and/or mainmast and fore-and-aft rigging on the mizzenmast was known as "brig-rigged." If all the masts were rigged fore-and-aft, the ship was "sloop-rigged."

Barquentine

Barquentines (barqs, barks, barques) were small trading vessels with three masts; they were square-rigged on the foremast and fore-and-aft rigged on the mainmast and mizzenmast. The ships were hardy workhorses, but while their slowness made them good targets for plundering, they held little attraction as a pirate vessel.

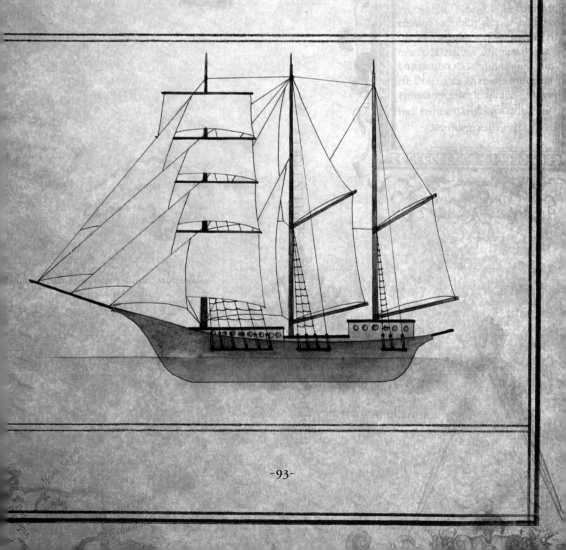

Brigantine

The brigantine (or brig) was commonly used in coastal American trading. It had two masts, with a square-rigged mainmast and a mizzenmast with a fore-and-aft-rigged mainsail and a square-rigged topsail. Brigs were up to eighty feet long, weighed about 150 tons, and could carry a hundred men and ten cannons. The brig was a very versatile vessel; the square-rigging made it good at sailing in quartering winds, while with the fore-and-aft rigging it excelled when sailing to windward.

Captain Hook's vessel in *Peter Pan*, the *Jolly Roger*, is a brigantine.

Caravel

Developed during the fifteenth century, this small, fast trading ship originally combined a stern rudder with lateen-rigged sails that later became square-rigged. These ships were used by Spanish explorers and could be handled easily by a small crew.

Carrack

The introduction of permanent fighting platforms and artillery led to the development of large ships called carracks that succeeded the caravel and were the forerunners of the galleon. The carrack was the backbone of European merchant fleets trading on long voyages to India, China, and the Americas. They had three masts: square-rigged fore- and mainmasts, and a lateen-rigged mizzenmast.

Crumster

This was a variation on the hoy *(see page 101)*; it lacked speed but it could carry lots of loot and the gun deck could carry up to sixteen guns. It had three masts, with the mizzenmast carrying a lateen or gaff sail. The crumster could be used as a warship to protect a fleet of galleons.

Galleot

This is a small version of the galley that was easier to man and maintain. Galleots were faster than the bigger war galleys and were popular with the Mediterranean pirates.

Galleon

Galleons were designed to carry large loads across the Atlantic to and from the Spanish colonies. Most galleons had four masts. The mast at the back was called the bonadventure mast and had lateen-rigged sails. Galleons were sleek, relatively fast (eight knots), and well-armed, but not without their drawbacks. The hull sloped inwards as it rose and tapered into a top deck. While this meant that the weight of the cannons was close to the centerline of the ship for added stability, other factors reduced its stability, such as its small keel and high castles at the forepeak and stern. The result was a ship that could carry 200 men, forty paying passengers, and seventy-four cannons, but which pitched and rolled considerably, making it more vulnerable to attack from smaller, more stable ships. Nevertheless, galleons were formidable fighting ships and even had blades on their outermost yardarms to slash the sails of ships that came too close.

If pirates succeeded in capturing a galleon they would strip it down, removing the high castles to reduce weight and increase speed. The superstructures of English galleons were already much lower than their Spanish counterparts, so they were more stable and more maneuverable. The typical Spanish galleon weighed between 300 and 500 tons; many English race-built galleons, such as Francis Drake's *Golden Hind*, weighed only 120 tons.

Galley

This was a long, square-rigged vessel with a row of between twenty and forty oars. Each oar was pulled by two or three men, who were either captives or pirates. The oars meant that the galley could attack from the leeward side or escape into the wind. Galleys were used by the Barbary corsairs, who favored them for their ability to bombard the enemy while keeping out of the angle of fire of the enemy's broadsides. A forecastle at the back carried several forward-facing guns and some swivel guns. The galley pointed its bow at the enemy to fire, thereby making itself into the smallest possible target.

Captain Kidd, one of the few pirates to commission his own vessel, chose the galley design and called his ship the *Adventure Prize*. It carried thirty-four guns and initially a crew of seventy men. Under full sail and oar it could reach fourteen knots despite a weight of nearly 300 tons (its weight was due to its ribs being closer together than normal, which made it better able to withstand cannon strikes).

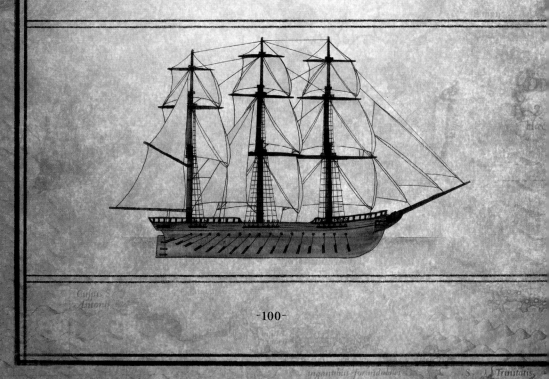

Hoy

The hoy was a version of the sloop that could be either sloop-rigged or square-rigged with a gaff sail. Hoys were used for transporting cargo over short distances, but they would not have been used for long voyages and had only a handful of cannons. Pirates in a hoy would adopt hit-and-run tactics, making a strike and then sailing quickly back to shallow water to hide their spoils.

Junk

The universal maritime vessel in the Far East, the junk was originally developed during the Han dynasty and became the longest-serving ship in human history. Junks were fast and highly maneuverable. The largest pirate junks were over 100 feet long with four masts, but most were smaller (about forty feet long) with one or two masts. The sails were made of bamboo matting, but rich warlords had sails of colored silk. They were cut elliptically, shaped with bamboo battens into a gentle curve, and could be angled to catch the wind. The battens made the sails very strong. Rigging was simple, reducing the number of ropes required. Other notable features included a high stern, a flat bow, and an adjustable rudder. Pirate junks had swivel guns called *lantaka*. Below deck, the ship was divided into cabins, where the whole family was quartered.

Man-of-War

The Royal Navy designed heavily-armed combat ships to suppress piracy. These men-of-war would often escort merchant ships, staying just out of sight beyond the horizon. They were known as corvettes if they had one deck, frigates if they had two, and ships of the line with three decks. Only the bravest pirates would attempt to capture a man-of-war; most steered well clear of them.

Schooner

This vessel had two masts which were usually both fore-and-aft rigged. It had a shallow draft, drawing only about five feet of water, so it could easily hide out in shallow water. It had a narrow hull and with a favorable wind could streak through the water at a speed of almost twelve knots. Its main drawback was a lack of hold space, which limited traveling range and the amount of plunder it could carry. It weighed about 100 tons, had eight cannons, and needed around seventy-five crew.

One of the most famous pirate vessels of fiction, the *Hispaniola*, which appears in Robert Louis Stevenson's *Treasure Island*, was a schooner.

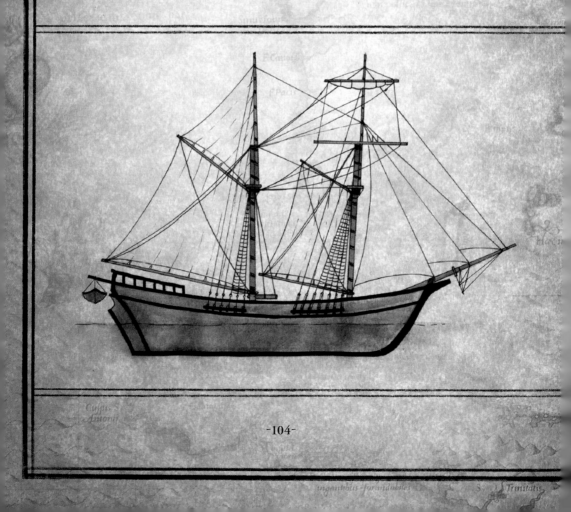

Shebec

Popular with Barbary pirates, the shebec (also xebec) was fast and large and had oars like a galley. Its three masts were usually lateen-rigged; it weighed up to 200 tons and could support up to twenty-four cannons, as well as 200 crew.

Ship

In the eighteenth century, the word ship had a more specific meaning than it does now. It referred to large vessels with three or more masts and square-rigging. The biggest of them were huge warships weighing over 200 tons and armed with up to forty guns. Many of the large merchant vessels were "ships," and they were captured and used by a large number of pirates.

Sloop

During the seventeenth and eighteenth centuries, the sloop was the most popular pirate vessel. It was a single-masted ship rigged fore-and-aft with a mainsail and a single foresail, or jib. It carried a vast amount of sail relative to its size, making it very fast. Records of pirate attacks in the Caribbean and North American coast between 1710 and 1730 show that over half were carried out by pirates in sloops; forty-five percent involved ships and only fifteen percent combined involved brigs, brigantines, and schooners.

Sloops varied in size from two-man turtle boats to Royal Navy men-of-war with twelve guns. In the eighteenth century, the word "sloop" referred to a range of smaller vessels, most of which were built in Bermuda and Jamaica, and were between thirty-five and sixty-five feet long with up to twelve guns on the single deck. These highly-regarded vessels were built with red cedar and had a steeply-raked mast.

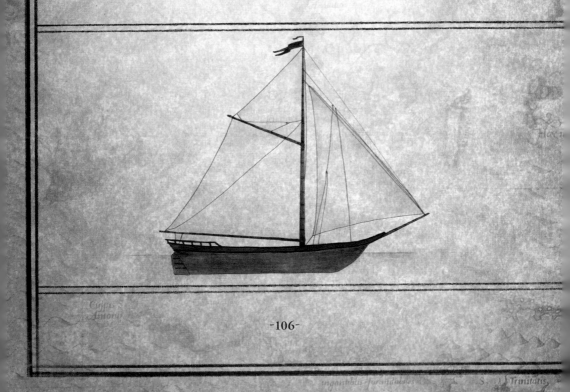

PIRATE FLAGS

The purpose of the pirate flag, or "Jolly Roger," was to terrify victims into surrendering. The violence meted out by pirates to those they conquered ensured that whenever a crew was approached by a ship flying one, they knew that if they resisted and lost, they would suffer a terrible fate.

While many flags used common symbols such as the skull and cross-bones, or crossed swords, they also had specific designs to identify particular pirates. The fiercer the pirate's reputation, the more likely that the ship would surrender. Some pirates, such as the French buc-caneer L'Olonnais, killed their victims regardless of whether they put up a fight, so sometimes fighting was the only option.

The name "Jolly Roger" is thought to have come from the French *joli rouge*, which means "pretty red," an ironic reference to the blood-stained rag that early privateers and buccaneers used as a flag dur-ing the seventeenth century. Also, rouge was associated with English vagrancy laws, and the name Roger became synonymous with rogues, vagabonds, or beggars. In addition, "Old Roger" was another name for the Devil. Pirates were evil "Sea Beggars," so it was fitting that they should adopt this symbol.

The red color signaled that no mercy would be given; in short, the fight would be bloody and to the death. These red flags were often flown alongside a national flag. In 1694, the English Admiralty made it obligatory for all privateers to fly a red privateering flag called the "Red Jack."

Pirates could lure a ship into thinking it was safe by posing as a privateer flying the same national flag (since privateers were only supposed to attack foreign ships). Similarly, a pirate ship could fly a fake national flag to avoid being attacked. After legitimate privateering opportunities petered out in the early eighteenth century, many privateers turned to piracy and used the old symbols of their trade.

The first customized black Jolly Roger was used by French privateer turned pirate Emanuel Wynne, in 1700. His flag featured a skull and crossbones and an hourglass to signify that time was running out for his victims. Some flags used wings to represent time "flying away." Other common symbols included images from gravestones, allegorical paintings, and church carvings. Thomas Tew's flag depicted an arm holding a sword, to represent a tough fight.

Only Edward England used the original single full-frontal skull and cross bones; all other pirates added or changed features. For example, Christopher Condent had three skulls and crossbones on a triangular banner, while the skull on Henry Avery's flag is shown in side profile and wearing an earring.

Many pirates simply used a large black flag without any symbols. When Howell Davis took up piracy he didn't have a Jolly Roger, so he flew "a dirty tarpaulin, by way of a black flag, they having no other," and it sent out the desired message.

While everyone was familiar with the symbols that were used, some flags were highly personalized. For example, one of Bartholomew Roberts's flags showed a pirate holding a sword and standing on two skulls, with the initials ABH and AMH. These stood for "A Barbadian's Head" and "A Martiniquan's Head," in reference to his long-standing grudge against the inhabitants of these islands. It sent out a clear message that if anyone from those parts of the Caribbean offered resistance, they would be shown no mercy. In 1720 Roberts made good on his threat by hanging the governor of Martinique from a yardarm. Roberts's other flag showed him and a skeleton holding an hourglass.

Other pirate flags showed men toasting or dancing a jig with Death; both symbols were meant to demonstrate that the pirates weren't afraid of dying and were careless of their fate. Edward Low's flag was a red skeleton on a black background.

The most feared flag of all was Blackbeard's. It showed a horned skeleton pointing a spear at a red bleeding heart. The message was unambiguous: resist and no one will be spared a slow and painful death.

Famous Pirate Flags

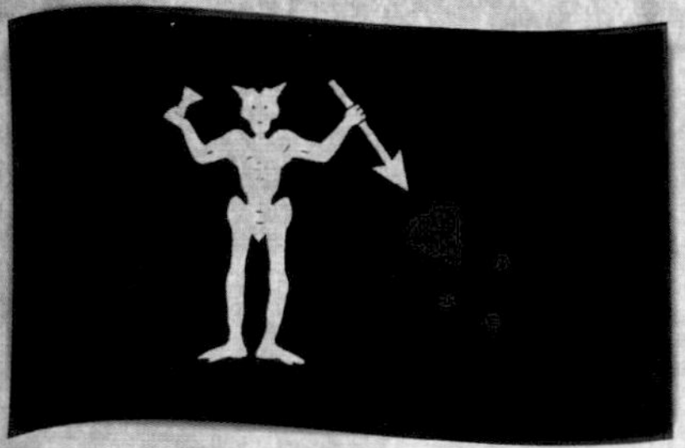

Edward Teach
("Blackbeard")

Stede Bonnet

Christopher Condent

Captain Dulaien

Edward England

Henry Avery

Famous Pirate Flags

Edward Low

Christopher Moody

John Quelch

John Rackham
(Calico Jack)

Batholomew Roberts
(Black Bart)

Thomas Tew

PIRATE CLOTHING

From the early fourteenth century, in order to maintain appropriate distinctions between levels of society, many European countries passed sumptuary laws that were strictly enforced. They were intended to emphasize the difference between the nobility and the commoners by restricting what commoners could wear and eat, where they could live, and how long their swords and daggers could be. This was, of course, motivated by upper-class arrogance, and the concern that allowing people to wear what they pleased could result in moral chaos, since a milkmaid might pass for a duchess with disastrous results. However, it was also to safeguard against young gentlemen overextending themselves financially to appear richer. The Enforcing Statutes of Apparel, issued at Greenwich, June 15, 1574, sets out the problem:

"The excess of apparel and the superfluity of unnecessary foreign wares thereto belonging now of late years is grown by sufferance to such an extremity that the manifest decay of the whole realm generally is like to follow (by bringing into the realm such superfluities of silks, cloths of gold, silver, and other most vain devices of so great cost for the quantity thereof as of necessity the moneys and treasure of the realm is and must be yearly conveyed out of the same to answer the said excess) but also particularly the wasting and undoing of a great number of young gentlemen, otherwise serviceable, and others seeking by show of apparel to be esteemed as gentlemen, who, allured by the vain show of those things, do not only consume themselves, their goods, and lands which their parents left unto them, but also run into such debts and shifts as

they cannot live out of danger of laws without attempting unlawful acts, whereby they are not any ways serviceable to their country as otherwise they might be."

Men or women with ideas above their station could find themselves imprisoned or in the stocks. In France, Louis XIV banned the importation of costly fabric, making it illegal for those of low birth to wear fabrics such as silk, satin, velvet, brocade, taffeta, lace, and gold- or silver-threaded cloth. "Expensive" colors (i.e., the dyes to create them were scarce) such as gold, silver, purple, and scarlet were also banned, as were jewelry such as gold, silver, earrings, necklaces, and gemstones. Thus, pirates wore what nobles wore—fine clothes, earrings, etc.—to enrage and antagonize their betters whom they so despised.

When the booty was shared after a raid, fine clothing was auctioned off among the pirates and the money went into the ship's coffers to buy supplies. Fine clothes were highly sought after items of plunder, and competition for the best would be fierce.

A pirate out on the town might typically wear a shirt of fine linen or silk, with lace cuffs. Satin breeches were worn over white cotton or wool stockings that reached above the knee. Over this he would wear a plain or heavily embroidered thigh-length waistcoat made of fine satin or brocade. Around the neck was worn a fine-linen neckstock or a white strip of pleated lace called a jabot. The outfit was completed with an ornate surcoat with long, wide cuffs that extended to the mid-calf.

Headwear wasn't restricted to the famous pirate tricorne; other wide-brimmed or cocked hats were worn and they might be decorated with jewelry and the feathers of exotic birds. Colorful exotic birds have long been part of pirate mythology, but they weren't a fashion accessory, and pirates did not keep them as pets. A pirate would walk around town with one perched on his shoulder to advertise that it was for sale.

Jewelry was not restricted to an earring. Much gold and many gems being transported in merchant ships along the Spanish Main had already been fashioned into jewelry, because the import tax was cheaper than that charged on items such as gold ingots or coins and gems. So when trade ships were raided, much of this jewelry ended up in pirate hands, to be worn or sold.

Bartholomew Roberts was one of the best-dressed of his fellow pirates. A contemporary described him as "dressed in a rich crimson damask waistcoat and breeches, a red feather in his hat, a gold chain round his neck, with a diamond cross hanging to it." Outsiders they may have been, but pirates certainly conformed to ideas of their time about what constituted desirable apparel. Others, such as Blackbeard, were more interested in scaring than impressing people. He tied ropes in his long hair and set fire to them when he went into battle.

On board, ship clothing was altogether more functional. Fancy lace cuffs and damask waistcoats were impractical. The coat worn on board had a short, straight cut and became known as a "fearnought" or a "bum-freezer." At sea, knitted caps, knotted scarves, or wide-brimmed hats, were favored over the tricorne.

Since many pirates were recruited as unemployed, mutinied, or cap-tured seaman, they often wore the clothing that had been prescribed for them on board their civilian ship. Pirates who sailed after 1628 might wear a set of clothing called "slops," which the British Admi-ralty created for the regular press-ganged sailor. This included a canvas doublet and breeches, knitted caps, linen shirts, cotton waistcoats, and stockings.

Since many of a pirate's plundered clothes were ill-fitting and of clash-
ing colors, the term "motley crew" came into use to refer to groups of
idiosyncratically dressed pirates (motley being a multi-colored woven
fabric).

Another popular style of
breeches was baggy "petticoat"
breeches, which increasingly
became longer, looser cut, and
more open, and developed
into the earliest examples of
trousers.

Large bucket-topped boots
may have been worn by some
pirate captains, but on the
whole pirates went around
in bare feet on board, so that
they could climb easier and
grip the deck. Usually, they
wore simple laced or buckled
shoes that were "straight,"
which means that both shoes
were identical, left and right.

Chapter 5

Rogue's Gallery

From the Caribbean to the Indian Ocean and the South China Seas, many pirates have made their fortunes and their reputations. Here are over a dozen notorious pirates whose names struck fear into the hearts of the bravest of sea captains.

BARBAROSSA BROTHERS (1470S–1518/1547)

Two Greek brothers, Aruj and Hizir Rais, were notorious pirates along the Barbary Coast during the sixteenth century and became famous for extending Islamic influence to the whole of the Mediterranean.

They were born in Greece in the 1470s. Their mother hailed from the Aegean island of Lesbos, a well-known pirate haven. Their father was a retired Ottoman soldier turned potter, who traded with his own small galleot.

Aruj was serving on his father's galleot when he was captured by a large galley belonging to the Christian Knights of Rhodes. He served as a galley slave for several months, but was later released by Egyptian forces and brought to Alexandria, where he was joined by Hizir. The two brothers then set up a pair of corsair galleys funded by an Egyptian emir and proved themselves to be formidable raiders. The smaller of the galleys had seventeen oars with two men on each oar, while the larger ship had two decks and twenty-six oars. The brothers didn't use Christian slaves for oarsmen; instead they used Turkish or Muslim freemen, which meant that captain and crew were united in a common goal. Aruj had a striking red beard and Hizir had an auburn one, thus each was nicknamed "Barbarossa" (red beard).

Hizir

Their first big success was the capture of the Pope's own trading galley off Elba. According to sixteenth-century historian Diego Haedo, "The wonder and astonishment that this notable exploit caused in Tunis, and even in Christendom, is not to be expressed, nor how celebrated Aruj Rais was become from that very moment."

In 1505, the brothers moved to the western Mediterranean and used the island port of Djerba as a base to offload their considerable plunder from papal galleys and Spanish merchants and warships. Within five years they were among the richest men in the Mediterranean and commanded a fleet of eight galleots.

After falling out with the Sultan of Tunis in 1511, they moved their base to Djidjelli near Algiers and attacked many coastal towns and forts. In 1512, Aruj lost his left arm while attacking a Spanish fort on the North African coast. With Aruj incapacitated, the Genoese Senate sent a fleet of twelve large galleys to destroy the brothers; Hizir fought them with six galleots, but was forced to retreat. Two years later, after regrouping their fleet, they attacked the fort a second time, but failed again when Spanish reinforcements arrived. From then on they focused much of their aggression on the Spanish and attacked Spanish coastal settlements.

Barbary Coast States

Aruj revolted against the Sultan of Algiers in 1516, killing him and assuming his title. He spent two years holding off the Spanish, who controlled Algiers Bay and Oran. Spain sent a powerful fleet with 10,000 soldiers led by Admiral Diego de Vera to wipe out the Turkish presence on the African coast. But Aruj attacked this force from land as soon as they reached the coast. The Bishop of Pamplona described the carnage: "Barbarossa came out . . . and fell upon them with his forces shouting war cries. So great was the fear that his very name inspired that the Spaniards were totally routed, with very little loss to the attackers. Almost effortlessly the Turks and their followers killed over 3,000 men as well as capturing 400." On its retreat to Spain, most of the Spanish fleet was destroyed by a storm. Aruj became the undeniable master of the North African coast.

Aruj was finally halted in 1518 by a six-month siege in the town of Tlemcen. He was killed while trying to escape and Hizir assumed control. Hizir continued to resist the Spanish around Algiers and earned himself the title Khair-ed-Din ("the gift of God"). He forged an alliance with the Ottoman emperor and was officially made the Sultan of Algiers. He sacked Majorca and Nice, and defeated a Christian galley fleet in the Mediterranean. By the time of his death in 1547, the brothers' exploits were, according to Ernle Bradford, "to determine the pattern of life and trade in the Mediterranean until the early nineteenth century."

SIR FRANCIS DRAKE (1540-1596)

Sir Francis Drake is the best-known English sailor of the Elizabethan era. He led the English assault on the Spanish during the six-teenth century and made nu-merous sorties to the Spanish Main to attack shipping and disrupt the flow of wealth from the New World to Spain.

He was born in Tavistock, Devon in 1540, the son of a farmer. He took to the sea in his early teens on a cargo barque, which he later captained. In his early twenties he made his first expedition to the New World with a cargo of slaves from Africa. The expedition was attacked by Spaniards and only two ships survived. This experience inspired Drake with a life-long hatred of the Spanish.

Drake led his first expedition in 1570, and two more in 1571 and 1572. During the latter expedition, he captured Nombre de Dios on the Isthmus of Panama. Several setbacks followed, but he succeeded in capturing the next annual convoy to the Spanish Main and returned to England with his treasure. Queen Elizabeth I had just signed a temporary truce with King Philip II of Spain and refused to condone Drake's activities publicly. However, secretly she was quite happy for him to sail around the Spanish Main for the glory of England, and she supported him financially on his 1577 expedition. On this trip he had five ships, led by the flagship *Pelican*, which he later renamed the *Golden Hind*. The fleet was supposed to sail to Africa, then to South America, but a storm at Cape Horn changed his plans. Drake sailed on his own to South America and attacked Chile. He raided many Spanish settlements, including Valparaiso, Lima, and Arica, but according to researcher Oliver Seeler, "The plundering was remarkable for its restraint; neither the Spanish nor the natives were intentionally harmed, there was very little violence, and there were very few casualties."

In 1579 he attacked the Spanish galleon *Cacafuego*, which yielded the richest haul of treasure that England had ever captured. He also landed near present-day San Francisco and claimed the area for England, naming it "Nova Albion" which is Latin for "New England." He then sailed west across the Pacific and reached England in September 1580, becoming the first Englishman to circumnavigate the globe. He was now a very wealthy celebrity. The Queen knighted him the following year, and he became the Mayor of Plymouth and a Member of Parliament. The Queen had invested 1,000 crowns in the expedition and she received 47,000 crowns in return, more than enough to pay off the national debt. She allowed Drake to keep 10,000 crowns with which he bought a large estate called Buckland Abbey.

Five years later Drake led a fleet of thirty-five ships to the Spanish Main on an official privateering expedition. Although the expedition didn't yield significant financial reward, Drake captured Santa Domingo in Hispaniola, Cartagena in Venezuela, and St. Augustine in Florida.

In 1587, Drake entered the port of Cadiz and destroyed thirty ships from the Spanish Armada, delaying the sailing of the Armada by a year. When it set sail in 1588, it was defeated by the English fleet, and Drake, now vice admiral of the British fleet, was instrumental in this historic victory. A famous anecdote tells how he was playing bowls on Plymouth Hoe when he learned of the approach of the Spanish Armada, whereupon he declared that there was plenty of time to finish his game before beating the Spaniards. He returned to the Spanish Main in 1595 to capture Panama but failed. He caught a fever and died the following year, a national hero to the English and "El Dragón," the pirate, to the Spanish.

HENRY MORGAN (1635-1688)

Henry Morgan was the most successful of all buccaneers. He terrorized the Spanish Main during a career that lasted a decade. Unlike most buccaneers, who usually died on the job, Morgan was able to retire a wealthy man and live off his spoils.

His fame is due in part to Alexander Exquemelin's *The Buccaneers of America*, which vividly describe his raids. But his achievements were prodigious by any standard.

Little is known of his early life. He was born in Wales, the son of a farmer, and spent some time in Barbados as an indentured servant before moving to Jamaica. He became a militia officer in 1662, and later that year a privateer.

In 1664 Morgan set out on a two-year buccaneering expedition during which he plundered three cities. He returned to Jamaica, bought a plantation, and married.

In 1668 he was ordered by the Governor of Jamaica, Thomas Modyford, to "draw together the English privateers and take prisoners of the

Spanish nation, whereby you may gain information of that enemy." He was allowed to plunder Spanish ships, but not to attack Spanish cities with his ships. His commission didn't mention attacks by land, which Morgan favored because all the booty went to him, whereas half the booty from sea attacks had to be given to the English government. However, attacking cities was still technically illegal.

He gathered a fleet of ten ships and 500 men and sailed to Cuba where they marched on Porte Principe. He locked the inhabitants in a church and, according to Exquemelin, the captives were "pained and plagued by unspeakable tortures" to reveal their treasures. The spoils of this raid were poor, so Morgan attacked Porto Bello in July 1668, despite the fact that it was defended by three massive forts. Morgan knew that the forts were poorly manned, so he took them easily. During this campaign he and his crew used women and nuns as human shields, sending them to the fortress walls with ladders. After negotiations, Morgan returned the cities for a ransom of 100,000 pesos and sailed back to Jamaica.

In 1670 Morgan set out from Hispaniola with thirty-six ships and 1,800 men to attack the city of Panama, a desirable Spanish possession prized for its rich merchants and mining wealth. First, Morgan and his crew took the Caribbean island of Old Providence, then they sailed up the Chagres River, and marched overland to Panama. The city was burned to the ground and Morgan returned to Jamaica with a large fortune in slaves, precious metals, and jewels. He made £1,000 from the Panama expedition alone. After spending some years in London, where he was knighted, he returned to Jamaica where he was made governor. He died there eight years later.

FRANÇOIS L'OLONNAIS (C.1635-1667)

Born Jean David Nau, this notorious pirate gained his nickname from his birthplace, Les Sables D'Olonne, in Brittany. One of the most bloodthirsty and cruelest buccaneers of all time, François L'Olonnais hated Spaniards so much he gained another epithet, *Fleau des Espagnols*—the Flail of the Spaniards.

He sailed to the Caribbean in 1650 where he spent three years as an indentured servant on Spanish plantations, before joining a group of cattle hunters at Hispaniola, then turning to piracy. He based himself at Tortuga and was given captaincy of a ship by the French governor.

He attacked Spanish ships with unprecedented brutality. Whenever he captured a ship, he would massacre the entire crew, except for two or three men whom he would set free so that they could spread the news of his fearsome treatment of prisoners. This meant that crews rarely surrendered, and that he had to fight them "until they could fight no more, for he granted Spaniards little mercy." Once he attacked a small

Cuban port, killing all his prisoners except one. He gave this man a letter to deliver to the governor of Havana with the warning that he would kill every Spaniard he captured.

According to Exquemelin, "it was the custom of L'Olonnais that, having tortured any persons and they not confessing, he would instantly cut them in pieces with his hanger [cutlass] and pull out their tongues."

In 1667 when war broke out between France and Spain, L'Olonnais attacked Spanish towns in Venezuela. He sailed with a fleet of eight ships and 700 men to the treasure city of Maracaibo. The fort that protected the city was thought to be impregnable, but L'Olonnais attacked from the landward side and captured it within a few hours. He then rounded up many of the citizens who had fled to apparent safety in the woods, and tortured a group of women and children to make them tell him where treasure was hidden. Most of the treasure had already been moved across Lake Maracaibo to the town of Gibraltar, which was protected by hundreds of Spanish soldiers. This didn't deter L'Olonnais; forty of his men were killed and thirty wounded, but they killed over 500 Spaniards while taking the town. They spent a month there, then returned to Maracaibo to extort 20,000 pieces-of-eight in return for leaving the town's buildings standing. They sailed back to Tortuga with jewels, silverware, slaves, and 260,000 pieces-of-eight, the majority of which they quickly squandered in the local taverns and brothels.

The following year, L'Olonnais sailed to Lake Nicaragua to plunder its silver wealth. However, his ship was becalmed and drifted into the

Gulf of Honduras, where he pillaged several Indian villages before reaching Puerto Caballos.

After torturing the inhabitants, he made two prisoners lead him to the nearby town of San Pedro. Exquemelin describes how L'Olonnais punished his hapless guides after they were ambushed en route: "He ripped open one of the prisoners with his cutlass, tore the living heart out of his body, gnawed at it, and then hurled it in the face of one of the others."

After burning San Pedro to the ground, he captured a Spanish galleon which he later ran aground off the coast of Honduras. He headed for the Isthmus of Darien, but on the way he was ambushed by cannibalistic Indians, and L'Olonnais suffered a fate similar to that which he had inflicted on so many of his prisoners. The Indians "tore him in pieces alive, throwing his body limb by limb into the fire, and his ashes into the air; to the intent no trace nor memory might remain of such an infamous, inhuman creature."

Caribbean Sea

Maracaibo

Venezuela

Captain (William) Kidd (1645-1701)

William Kidd was one of the most notorious pirates who sailed the seas. He was born in Scotland and rose through the ranks to become a sea captain. He became an English privateer with a mission to loot all the French ships he could find. For this job, he was given a state-of-the-art vessel, the *Adventure Galley*, which weighed 237 tons, had thirty-four cannons, and was manned by a crew of eighty handpicked from the roughest bunch of cutthroats New York could offer (the Royal Navy having taken the most experienced and reliable members of his original crew).

Kidd set sail in 1696 from New York and headed for Madagascar. He didn't encounter any French ships during the voyage, and the crew became mutinous, since they had gained no plunder. They wanted Kidd to attack any ship they found, but he refused.

Finally, with the crew on the brink of mutiny, Kidd killed his gunner, William Moore, in a brawl, but it didn't stop a mass desertion. With the remaining crew, Kidd then ran amok, doing precisely what he had refused to do before the mutiny: attack all ships.

In January of 1698 he made a decision that would later cost him his life. He attacked the huge 400-ton *Quedah Merchant*. It was an amazing feat, since the vessel feigned surrender then fired its cannons as Kidd approached. However, a lucky sea swell made the cannons miss their target and Kidd boarded the ship to claim one of the greatest pirate treasures ever.

While he was repairing the *Quedah Merchant* (which he had renamed the *Adventure Prize*), he met and fell in love with a woman from Barneget named Amanda. He resolved to retire from piracy and settle down with her, so he stole treasure from his crew and buried much of it on Gardiner's Island. His furious crew sailed to New York and told the authorities where they could find and arrest him.

Kidd had attacked the ship legitimately, since it had French papers, but unluckily for him, most of the cargo belonged to the British East India Company. He had stolen from some of the most powerful people in the world, and they exerted all their influence to bring him to justice (even though he had originally enjoyed the support of rich and powerful backers such as William Coote, the Earl of Bellomont). He was deported to England to face trial for piracy and the murder of William Moore. Kidd was found guilty on both charges and sentenced to death. He was unable to prove that he was a legitimate privateer and not a pirate, because Bellomont destroyed the evidence–logbook and papers.

Before he was hanged he reportedly made this farewell speech:

My name was Captain Kidd,

When I sail'd, when I sail'd,

And so wickedly I did, God's laws I did forbid,

When I sail'd, when I sail'd.

I roam'd from sound to sound, And many a ship I found,

And then I sunk or burn'd, When I sail'd.

I murder'd William Moore, And laid him in his gore,

Not many leagues from shore, When I sail'd.

Farewell to young and old, All jolly seamen bold,

You're welcome to my gold, For I must die, I must die.

Farewell to Lunnon town, The pretty girls all round,

No pardon can be found, and I must die, I must die,

Farewell, for I must die. Then to eternity, in hideous misery,

I must lie, I must lie.

He was hanged on May 23, 1701. It took two attempts, because the rope broke. His dead body was dipped in tar, chained, and hung alongside the River Thames in London as a warning to other pirates.

Today, Captain Kidd is remembered as much for his buried treasure as for anything else. Some of his loot was discovered and dug up shortly after his death, but it is thought that the lion's share of his fortune still lies unclaimed somewhere up the Connecticut River.

THOMAS JONES (C.1670S-UNKNOWN)

Little is known about the early life of Thomas Jones. He was Welsh, and as a young man he fought on the side of James II against William III at the Battle of the Boyne in 1690, which led to his being exiled to Ireland. He escaped Ireland by becoming a privateer and was granted a Letter of Marque by King William to attack French shipping.

Jones commissioned a ship and arrived in the West Indies in 1692. During the next four years he operated as a pirate and by 1696 he was a very wealthy man. He bought a large estate in what is now Massapequa on Long Island. Jones Inlet on the South Bay and Jones Beach are both named for him.

Jones returned from his privateering exploits to become a prominent figure in New York society, but he spoke little about how he made his fortune. His family prospered, until after the American Revolution when Congress passed the "Act of Attainder" which was designed to confiscate all Loyalist property (Jones had supported the British and it was widely rumored that his estate had been a haven for British spies). Many members of his family went to Nova Scotia or returned to England, but Jones made a skillful deal with his neighbor, William Floyd, who was one of the signatories of the Declaration of Independence. Jones's son, David, married one of Floyd's daughters, and changed his name to Floyd-Jones. In return, Floyd engineered a special Act of Congress to exempt the Floyd-Jones estate from the Act of Attainder. The family kept the Jones money and David even became Speaker of the New York State Assembly.

Today, the Long Island estate is part of the National Park System. Jones's mansion still stands and some believe that his pirate treasure is buried somewhere on the estate. One disgruntled treasure hunter scratched this inscription on his gravestone:

Beneath this Stone

Repose the bones

Of Pirate Jones

This briny well

Contains the shell

The rest's in Hell!

BLACKBEARD (C.1680-1718)

Edward Drummond was one of the most feared and hated pirates of all time. He came to prominence as "Blackbeard," named for the long black beard that almost covered his entire face. When he attacked merchant ships he wove rope into his hair and set fire to it. His fearsome look struck terror into his crew as well as his enemies. One of his victims described him as "a tall, spare man with a very black beard which he wore very long." He tied his beard with black ribbons and wore six flintlock pistols across his chest.

If a ship surrendered he would board it, then plunder its valuables, rum, and weapons; if the crew resisted, he would kill or maroon them. In his short pirating career he killed hundreds of people and looted over forty ships. He was not the most brutal of pirates, nor was he the most prolific, but his demonic appearance ensured that his name and reputation would live on.

Little is known about Drummond's early life. He was born in Bristol, England and, after several years as a privateer, began pirating in 1716 as an ordinary crewmember aboard a Jamaican sloop commanded by

Benjamin Hornigold. The following year, Hornigold gave Drummond (who by now called himself Edward Teach) a small crew of his own and a captured sloop to command. They sailed together and became a formidable team. In November 1717, they captured a twenty-six-gun French vessel named the *Concorde*. Afterward, Hornigold retired under a British amnesty, but Blackbeard converted the *Concorde* into his flagship pirate vessel, boosting its firepower to forty guns. He renamed the ship the *Queen Anne's Revenge*. He established a base at New Providence and captured several ships before relocating to North Carolina, just before the arrival of Governor Rogers. His new base was on Ocracoke Island near Bath Towne.

In the Gulf of Mexico, Blackbeard encountered the ten-gun pirate sloop *Revenge* from Barbados, commanded by Stede Bonnet, an "amateur" pirate with a private (rather than a stolen) boat. Blackbeard teamed up with him, but soon relieved him of his command and made Bonnet a guest-prisoner on his own ship. By the spring of 1718, Blackbeard was in command of four pirate ships and over 300 men.

In May of 1718, Blackbeard blockaded the port of Charleston, South Carolina, where he captured eight vessels and a number of prominent citizens, whom he held for ransom. He then returned to Ocracoke, where the *Queen Anne's Revenge* ran aground on a sandbar. Twenty-five members of Blackbeard's crew joined Bonnet aboard the *Revenge*, which was renamed the *Royal James*.

Blackbeard sold his plunder, was granted a pardon by Governor Charles Eden, and bought a house. However, his obedience to the amnesty was short-lived. After Charles Vane visited Blackbeard and they caroused for a week, the locals became worried that the Carolinas were turning into a new pirate haven, so Governor Alexander Spotswood sent a Royal Navy crew commanded by Lieutenant Robert Maynard to ambush Blackbeard at Ocracoke in November 1718. Many of his pirates were in Bathe Towne, so Blackbeard was heavily outnumbered and fought the bloodiest battle of his career. Maynard and Blackbeard fought hand-to-hand, and Blackbeard is reported to have suffered five bullet wounds and two dozen sword cuts before he died. Maynard captured more pirates in Bath Towne before sailing back to Williamsburg with Blackbeard's head hanging from the bowsprit of his sloop.

"Calico" Jack Rackham (unknown-1720)

Although his plundering exploits were not as impressive as some of the greater pirates, "Calico" Jack's capture and trial turned him into a media sensation after it was discovered that two of his crew were women. He was named for the cheap and colorful calico (cotton) shirt and striped breeches that he always wore, rather than the silks and velvets favored by his contemporaries. His reputation as a womanizer exceeded his pirating exploits. According to pirate scholar David Cordingly, "There is no record of Calico Jack using torture or murder, and he seems to have gone out of his way to treat his victims with restraint."

Calico Jack was a small-time pirate operating throughout the Caribbean and the West Indies. Initially, he served as Captain Charles Vane's quartermaster. In November 1718 he took control of Vane's ship after a dispute during which the crew chose him over Vane, who had refused to attack a promising French man-of-war in the Windward Passage. Vane had approached the vessel thinking that it was a regular merchant ship, but discovered it was a man-of-war when it turned broadside. Vane ordered a withdrawal, and his men obeyed (since the

Captain cannot be challenged during engagement), but as soon as they were a safe distance away the crew relieved him of his command. Calico Jack turned the ship around, and attacked and defeated the French vessel.

Calico Jack was granted a King's Pardon in 1719 by Captain Woodes Rogers, the Governor of the Bahamas. Sources differ as to how this happened. Some say that he lost his ship after being surprised by two naval sloops while the crew were ashore, and was granted a pardon as part of a pirate amnesty; others say he sailed to New Providence and surrendered voluntarily.

Around this time he met and fell in love with Anne Bonny, a married woman. He also encountered another woman, Mary Read. According to Captain Charles Johnson, Read's mother had dressed her as a boy during childhood to defraud a relative. She escaped and joined the army, then was captured by pirates in the West Indies.

Rackham returned to piracy after stealing the sloop *Curlew* from Nassau harbor, and he set sail with both women on board. They only discovered each other's true identities after Anne made a pass at Mary. Then the trio sailed around off the coast of Cuba attacking small vessels, although true control of the vessel fell to the two women (no longer in disguise). Rackham, who resented Anne's indiscretions with other members of the crew, had begun seeking solace in the bottle.

In October of 1720, they were aboard the newly captured government ship the *William* when it was captured by a heavily armed privateer, Captain Jonathan Barnet. The entire crew, except for the two women, were incapacitated with drink and hiding below decks during the attack. Only the women resisted the attack, but they were quickly overpowered. The crew were taken to Jamaica for trial. Both women were reprieved when it was discovered that they were pregnant, but Rackham and the rest of his men were hanged the following month. Before Rackham's death, Anne told him disparagingly, "If you had fought like a man you wouldn't now have to die like a dog. Do straighten yourself up!"

Calico Jack's body was placed in an iron cage and hung from a gibbet on the islet of Deadman's Quay near Port Royal as an example to other would-be pirates.

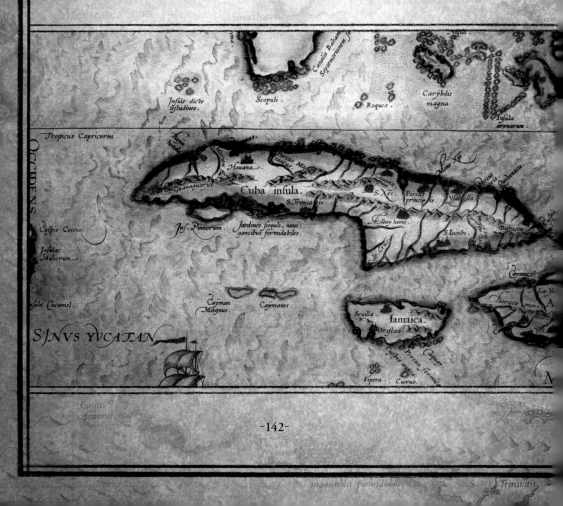

ANNE BONNY (1700-UNKNOWN)

Anne Bonny was one of the most famous female pirates in history. She served with "Calico" Jack Rackham and became a celebrity after their trial in 1720.

Anne Bonny was born near Cork, Ireland in 1700. She was the illegitimate daughter of lawyer William Cormac and Peg Brennan, the family maid. For a brief time Anne's father tried to pass Anne off as the son of a relative, but eventually the scandal forced him to leave Ireland with Peg and Anne. They moved to South Carolina where William practiced law and bought a plantation. When Anne was a teenager, Peg died and Anne became keeper of her father's house.

Captain Charles Johnson describes Anne as having "a fierce and courageous temper." He reports a rumor that she "killed an English servant-maid once in her passion with a case-knife," and he mentions in another story how "once, when a young fellow would have lain with her, against her will, she beat him so that he lay ill of it a considerable time."

When she was sixteen, Anne married sailor James Bonny, who hoped to inherit her father's plantation. But Anne's father disowned her, and the couple moved to New Providence in the Bahamas, where James made his living as an informer, turning pirates in to Governor Woodes Rogers. Meanwhile, Anne socialized with the pirate elite and had an affair with one of the richest men in the Caribbean, Chidley Bayard. She is thought to have fought a duel with her love rival, Spanish beauty Maria Vargas. At a ball, after the sister-in-law of Governor Lawes of Jamaica insulted her, she punched her in the mouth, knocking out two of her teeth.

Anne lost interest in Bayard and began an affair with "Calico" Jack Rackham, whom she went to sea with, dressed in men's clothes. According to Captain Johnson, "In all these expeditions, Anne Bonny kept him company, and when any business was to be done in their way, nobody was more forward or courageous than she. She was an expert with pistol and rapier and she was often a member of the boarding party when another ship was being taken."

On board Rackham's ship was another woman Mary Read, also dressed as a man. The women only discovered each other's true identities after Anne made a pass at Mary.

When Anne became pregnant, Rackham landed her in Cuba to give birth. She delivered the baby two months early and it died. Jack took her to New Providence where they took advantage of a pirate amnesty so that Anne could recuperate. While there, Anne saved the life of Governor Roberts by warning him of a plot to kill him. When Anne's husband James had her arrested for adultery with Jack Rackham, the Governor pardoned her on condition that Jack and James come to a divorce-by-sale arrangement, whereby Jack would buy her from her husband. Anne refused and the pair resumed pirating after stealing a merchant sloop, the *Curlew*, from New Providence harbor.

When Rackham and his crew were captured in 1720 and put on trial, Anne's father's reputation as an upstanding plantation owner stood in her favor, but the fact that she had committed adultery with Rackham was held against her. When it was discovered she was pregnant again, she was given a reprieve from her death sentence. It appears that she received several stays of execution before disappearing from official records. It is possible that her powerful father negotiated her release. Another story suggests that she was pardoned by Governor Lawes on condition that she leave the West Indies with the father of her child— not Jack Rackham, but a Dr. Michael Radcliffe.

MARY READ (UNKNOWN-1721)

Mary Read and Anne Bonny are two of the most famous female pirates in history. They served with "Calico" Jack Rackham and became celebrities after their trial in 1720.

Mary Read was born in England. Her young brother died shortly before Mary's birth, and her impoverished mother dressed Mary up as a boy and for several years attempted to pass her off as her dead brother in order to swindle a crown-a-week maintenance out of her husband's mother. When the old lady died, Mary, by now thirteen, was made to continue her charade when her mother put her forward as a footboy to a French lady. Mary ran away and, still dressed as a man, joined the Navy, then the cavalry. Daniel Defoe claims she fought in the Nine Years War, although it is more likely that she served in the War of the Spanish Succession. She gained a reputation as a brave fighter. According to Charles Johnson, "She behaved so well in several engagements that she earned the esteem of all her officers."

Mary fell in love with one of her fellow-soldiers, and "when her comrade was ordered put upon a party, she used to go without being commanded, and frequently run herself into danger, where she had no business, only to be near him." After she revealed her true identity to him and they married, she left the army, and they set up an inn together in Holland, where Mary lived as a woman for the first time in her life. When her husband died, Mary was forced to put on men's clothing again. She became a foot-soldier before sailing to the West Indies to seek her fortune.

In 1717 English pirates captured her ship and she joined them. After a while she gave up pirating under an amnesty, and became a privateer against the Spanish. As soon as the ship set sail, Mary and other crew members mutinied and returned to piracy with "Calico" Jack Rackham. She kept her female identity a secret until Anne Bonny made a pass at her, thinking she was a handsome youth. After this they became comrades, but Anne, who was married to Rackham, had to let him in on the secret after he became jealous of their friendship and threatened to run her through. Together, the threesome captured many ships in the West Indies.

In October of 1720, their ship, the *William,* was captured by a heavily armed privateer, Captain Jonathan Barnet, when the entire crew, except for the two women, were incapacitated with drink. Only the women resisted the attack, and they were quickly overpowered. The crew were taken to Spanish Town, Jamaica for trial. Both women were reprieved when it was discovered that they were pregnant.

At her trial Mary pleaded, like many pirates, that she had been co-erced into piracy, but many crewmates were willing to testify that "in times of action, no person amongst them were more resolute, or ready to board or undertake anything that was hazardous, as she and Anne Bonny."

Although her execution was postponed because of her pregnancy, she died shortly after her trial in prison of a violent fever.

Bartholomew Roberts (1682-1722)

Bartholomew Roberts was one of the most successful pirates of all time. During his thirty-month career he captured more than 400 ships and became the scourge of the Caribbean, the American colonies, and West Africa.

Roberts cut a dashing figure: although short, he was good-looking and always well-dressed. He was a man of contradictions, however: a devout Christian and teetotaler who forbade his men to gamble, he nevertheless displayed a ruthlessness that struck terror into all whom he conquered. He killed dissenting crewmembers and inflicted terrible tortures on numerous victims.

Born John Roberts in Pembrokeshire in South Wales, he was serving as mate on the slave ship *Princess*, when it was captured by Howell Davis and the crew of the *Royal Rover* in June 1719. Six weeks later Davis was killed in battle and Roberts was elected captain. At first he had been a reluctant pirate, but he told the crew "since he had dipped his hands in muddy water, and must be a pirate, it was better being a commander than a common man." He adopted the name Bartholomew and his subsequent exploits earned him the moniker "Black Bart."

Roberts first attacked the Portuguese settlement on Isle of Princes (now El Principe) to avenge the killing of Davis. Then he sailed to Brazil where he captured a Portuguese fleet escorted by two seventy-gun warships. The most heavily laden ship had 40,000 gold coins worth about $100,000. When he sailed for the Caribbean, his fleet was repulsed by the British Navy, so he proceeded to Newfoundland where he captured over 170 ships.

Roberts's reputation for ferociousness is illustrated by the reaction of merchant sailors when he sailed into Trepassey Bay with drums beating and his crew screaming. Roberts had one ten-gun sloop and sixty men, but the 1,200 terrified merchant sailors aboard twenty-two sloops anchored there immediately rowed to shore, leaving Black Bart to plunder freely. He captured a large brigantine, mounted her with twenty-eight guns, and renamed her the *Royal Fortune*, which became his new flagship. He then returned to the Caribbean and captured more than 100 ships, as well as the Governor of Martinique, whom he hanged from his own yardarm. Roberts almost single-handedly halted shipping to and from the Spanish Main.

His attempt to cross the Atlantic in 1720 proved disastrous, so he continued to plunder vessels around the Caribbean and inflict torture on his captives. The Governor of Bermuda reported that Roberts's French prisoners were "barbarously abused, some were whipped almost to death, others had their ears cut off, others they fixed to the yardarm and fired at them as a mark and all their actions looked like practicing of cruelty."

In 1721 his second attempt to cross the Atlantic was successful. He captured several slave ships off the coast of West Africa, including the *Onslow* of the Royal Africa Company, which he also renamed the *Royal Fortune*. Then he captured six ships off the Ivory Coast.

Roberts's reign of terror ended on February 10, 1722, when the *HMS Swallow* fired a broadside of grapeshot at close range while the ship was anchored off Cape Lopez in Gabon, killing him. The crew threw his body into the water to keep it from being captured and surrendered after a three-hour battle.

The subsequent trial was the most significant pirate trial of the time, with fifty-four of Roberts's men hanged, thirty-seven sentenced to hard labor, and seventy black pirates sold into slavery.

EDWARD ENGLAND (C.1695-1720)

Edward England was a brave and skillful pirate, but the leniency with which he treated those he conquered ultimately lead to his downfall. Captain Johnson, in *A General History of the Robberies and Murders of the Most Notorious Pyrates*, saw piracy as an unlikely choice for England. He describes him as "one of these men who seemed to have a great deal of good nature," and he muses that "it is surprising that men of good understanding should engage in a course of life that so much debases human nature, and sets them upon a level with the wild beasts . . ."

England was born Edward Seegar in Ireland, and became a pirate in 1717 after a Jamaican sloop he was serving on was captured by the pirate Christopher Winter in the Caribbean and he was pressed into service. He changed his surname and stayed with Winter until July 1718, when he captured a sloop and sailed off with his own crew. He crossed the Atlantic and captured several ships off the West African coast. One of them, the *Pearl*, he renamed the *Royal James* and made his flagship. Another ship, the *Victory*, he gave to John Taylor, one of his crewmen.

England and Taylor captured ten ships between the River Gambia and Cape Coast, four of which they burned. They kept two, the *Mercury* and the *Katherine*, and renamed them the *Queen Anne's Revenge* and the *Flying King*, respectively. These two ships left England's fleet and sailed to the Caribbean, but were captured by the Portuguese off the coast of Brazil. Thirty-eight of the crew were hanged.

Meanwhile, England sailed around the Cape of Good Hope and put ashore in Madagascar, where his crew careened the ships and, according to Captain Johnson, "lived there very wantonly for several weeks, making free with the Negro women, and committing such outrageous acts, that they came to an open rupture with the natives, several of whom were killed, and one of their towns they set on fire." Then they sailed off to the northwest coast of India and captured a thirty-four-gun square-rigged Dutch ship which England renamed the *Fancy* and made his flagship.

In August 1720 England engaged in a sea battle that would cause his crew to mutiny. Sailing in the *Fancy*, he encountered a heavily armed English East Indiaman, the *Cassandra*, captained by James Macrae. The battle lasted for several hours with both ships sustaining repeated broadside attacks. England finally gained the upper hand and Macrae sailed to shore and hid there for ten days. Meanwhile, England plundered the *Cassandra's* holds, which were filled with treasure totaling £75,000, the equivalent of tens of millions of dollars today.

Short of food and water, Macrae and his crew came out of hiding and gambled on being spared at England's hands. Over ninety of

England's crew had been killed during the battle, and there was great resentment among them when England set Macrae and his men free. Taylor quickly raised a group of mutineers to remove England from power and they marooned him on the island of Mauritius off the coast of Madagascar. (One of the men he was marooned with—described by Captain Johnson as "a man with a terrible pair of whiskers and a wooden leg, being stuck round with pistols"—is widely believed to have been the inspiration for the character of Long John Silver in *Treasure Island*.) England and his men made a small raft from scraps of wood and managed to sail to St. Augustine's Bay in Madagascar, where England lived out his last days begging for food.

JEAN LAFITTE (C.1780-1826/1840)

Jean Lafitte is a man of contradictions. During his life he was known by a number of nicknames, including "The Buccaneer," "The King of Barataria," "The Terror of the Gulf," and "The Hero of New Orleans." He could speak four languages and was very well-read and well-dressed. Jack C. Ramsay's description in *Jean Lafitte, Prince of Pirates* shows he was a lady's man: "Some considered him a rapacious rogue, a man of unmitigated violence. Others, many of whom were young women, regarded him as a charming person. He was seductive, perhaps deceptive, but always elegantly gracious."

Lafitte was a pirate in the Gulf of Mexico and, with his brother, ran a blacksmith business, from 1809 to 1814, as a front for an extensive smuggling operation. They led a group of a thousand pirates and smugglers based in Barataria Bay, south of New Orleans, but claimed never to have attacked an American ship.

Little is known of his early life. He is thought to have been born in France to a French father and a Spanish mother. He established his smuggling kingdom in the vast marshland of Louisiana after the

Louisiana Purchase of 1803. Washington authorities left the inhabitants of this untamed wetland area of swamps and bayous to fend for themselves, so Lafitte's merchandise was essential to the survival of citizens of New Orleans and its surroundings. Lafitte created a sophisticated transportation infrastructure, widening waterways, and digging canals. "Gigantic barges, one-hundred-feet long, were hewn from raw cypress trunks and shuttled back and forth almost daily to New Orleans, loaded with men and merchandise."

In 1810 Lafitte and his pirates began raiding ships in the Gulf of Mexico. Because slave trading was by now illegal in Louisiana, he sold slaves to plantation owners at secret auctions. He and his brother were arrested by the governor of Louisiana in 1812 on charges of piracy, but they escaped. The governor put a price of $500 on his head, and Lafitte responded by putting a price of $5,000 on the head of the governor.

Then came the War of 1812. The British blockaded U.S. ports, captured Washington, D.C., and burned the White House. In 1814, the British tried to repeat their success at New Orleans, and offered Lafitte a pardon if he would help them. Instead, he informed the state authorities—who promptly sailed into Barataria Bay and captured most of his pirate fleet. The following year Lafitte was offered a truce if he would help General Andrew Jackson repel the British attempt to gain control of the entire Mississippi River at the Battle of New Orleans. Without Lafitte's pirate force, New Orleans would have fallen to the English, as Jackson's forces were outnumbered. Lafitte became a hero and was pardoned by President James Madison. Before Jackson left New Orleans, he wrote Lafitte a personal letter: "Sir, to one of those to

whom the country is most indebted, I feel great pleasure in giving this testimony of your worth, and to add the sincere promise of my private friendship and high esteem."

After his pardon, Lafitte and his brother stole a ship and sailed to the island of Galveston, Texas, where they established another pirate kingdom called "Campeche." By 1817, this new base supported twenty pirate ships and a booming market in slaves and contraband, which continued until 1820 when the *USS Enterprise* led a force against him and sacked Galveston. Lafitte escaped and either died in a hurricane in the Gulf of Mexico or, as claimed in a controversial manuscript which appeared in the 1950s, the *Journal of Jean Lafitte*, he returned to the United States under an alias and raised a family until his death in the 1840s.

His lost treasure, which has never been recovered, has entered into pirate folklore. He is reported to have hidden his vast wealth in several locations in the marshes and swamps around Galveston Bay. It is also suspected that it may have gone down with his ship.

CHENG I SAO (1785-1844)

Many historians consider Cheng I Sao to be the most successful pirate who ever lived. After the death of her husband Cheng I, who controlled the biggest pirate confederation in history along the coastal waters of the South China Sea, she took control through skillful political maneuvering and proved to be an outstanding leader. Her husband owed much of his success to her organizational and diplomatic skills. She eventually commanded 2,000 ships.

She began her career as a Cantonese prostitute named Shih Yang and married Cheng I in 1801. (Cheng I Sao means "wife of Cheng".) She and her husband adopted a son named Chang Pao, who, after her husband's death in 1807, became her lover. She appointed him leader of the Red Fleet, the most powerful of her six fleets.

Cheng I Sao developed a pirate code of conduct with punishments that were much harsher than those of Western pirates. Each pirate received two plundered pieces for every ten captured, and the rest was stored in warehouses to ensure that the fleet was always funded. Anyone who stole or failed to disclose booty was beheaded. Even disobeying orders was punishable by death. Raping a female captive led to the pirate's execution. Consensual sex with a captive led to beheading for the man, and the woman being cast overboard with weights attached to her feet. The punishment for being absent without leave was losing an ear.

Cheng I Sao ran a protection racket along the coast, and sailed deep upriver to sack villages inland. She meted out violent punishment to those who resisted her. In 1809 she beheaded eighty men from San-shan village and sold the women and children into slavery.

Her fleets were so large that the Chinese Imperial Navy could not defeat them. In January of 1808 the pirates fought head to head with government forces in Kwangtung waters, and Cheng I Sao captured so many junks that the government was forced to use private fishing vessels to continue.

Cheng I Sao's greatest threat came from a rival pirate named O-po-tae, who forced her fleet to retreat. He later sought pardon from the Impe-rial government and retired. When the Imperial Navy had sought help from the British and Portuguese in 1810, Cheng I Sao decided to retire from piracy, after negotiating an amnesty with the Governor General of Canton. Chang Pao, now Cheng I Sao's husband, surrendered the entire Red Fleet and became a pirate hunter, helping to break up the confederation.

Cheng I Sao turned to running a brothel, gambling den, and smug-gling ring in Guangzhou. She died a rich old woman.

Pirate Superstitions

All sailors were superstitious and pirates were no exception. Here are some of their common beliefs:

Black Cat

Black cats were thought to carry a gale in their tails, so a black cat frolicking on the deck was a sign that a gale was imminent.

Cutting Nails Or Hair

In Roman times, nails and hair were offered to the goddess Proserpine. Cutting nails or hair at sea was thought to enrage the god Neptune for offerings made to another god while in his domain.

Drown

The word "drown" was never mentioned at sea. Sailors thought it was futile to fight the sea, so most never learned how to swim.

Earrings

Pirates wore golden earrings because they were fashionable, but also in the belief that they gave them better eyesight and protected them from drowning.

Feathers

Pirates often wore feathers in their hats for superstitious reasons. They were thought to protect sailors from shipwreck, especially the feather of a wren slaughtered on New Year's Day, which held its power for a year. This belief led to the virtual extinction of wrens on the Isle of Man.

Flowers

Flowers were discouraged on board because they were associated with the funeral wreath of a dead man.

Friday

Friday was the unluckiest day to set sail, as it was the day Christ was crucified and the day Eve tempted Adam in the Garden of Eden. The British Navy attempted to eliminate this superstition by commissioning the *HMS Friday*, which had its keel laid on a Friday, its crew selected on a Friday, and a captain named Jim Friday. It set sail on a Friday—and was never seen again.

Looking Shoreward

It was bad luck to look shoreward after the ship left shore.

Porpoise

These fast-swimming blunt-snouted mammals brought good luck to a boat, and it was unlucky to kill one.

Rats

Rats are well known for leaving a sinking ship, so if large numbers of them were seen escaping, they were killed in an attempt to prevent misfortune.

Repairing Flags

To mend a flag on the quarterdeck was sure to bring bad luck.

Right Foot First

When boarding a ship, a pirate never put his left foot down first, as this brought disaster.

Seagull

Seagulls were believed to carry the souls of drowned men, so it was bad luck to shoot one.

Silver Coin

There's an old tradition of putting coins under the mast or embedding them in the keel as good luck charms for a successful voyage.

Whistling For The Wind

Sailors believed that the wind could be summoned by whistling softly, after first sticking a knife in the mast. Whistling on deck while the wind was already blowing was thought to bring a gale.

Women

Women aboard a ship were considered unlucky, although a naked woman was thought to calm the seas. This is why many ships had figureheads of a bare-breasted woman.

Pirate Legends

Superstitions and legends were a way of dealing with the danger inherent in a life at sea and helped pirates and sailors alike to make sense of a confusing and uncharted world.

DAVY JONES'S LOCKER

Davy Jones is a sailor's nickname for the devil of the sea, and his locker is the ocean bed. Someone who was "sent to Davy Jones's locker" was someone who had perished at sea. If a pirate was scared, he could be described as having the Davies or the Joneseys. To awaken Davy Jones was to cause a storm.

The first written reference to Davy Jones's Locker appears in *The Adventures of Peregrine Pickle,* by Tobias Smollet, in 1751: "This same Davy Jones, according to sailors, is the fiend that presides over all the evil spirits of the deep, and is often seen in various shapes, perching among the rigging on the eve of hurricanes, ship-wrecks, and other disasters to which sea-faring life is exposed, warning the devoted wretch of death and woe."

Smollet describes him as having saucer eyes, three rows of teeth, horns, a tail, and blue smoke coming from his nostrils.

The name Davy is either a corruption of "duppy," the ghost spirit that originated in West Indian folk tales; or it could refer to Saint David, the patron Saint of Wales, who was known as Dewi. Other sources cite a British pub owner who appeared in the 1594 song "Jones's Ale is Newe," and whom legend has it threw drunken sailors into his ale locker before dumping them at sea.

Some versions of the legend indicate that a sailor may choose to serve Davy Jones for 100 years in preference to death.

THE FLYING DUTCHMAN

According to pirate folklore, the *Flying Dutchman* is a ghost ship that can never return to shore and is forced to sail the ocean for an eternity with its crew of dead souls. There are numerous versions of the story. In some, the captain is allowed to return to shore once every hundred years to find a woman. In Richard Wagner's opera of the same name, it is every seven years. Anyone who sees the ship will die a horrible death.

In most versions of the legend, the ghost ship was the result of a captain trying to round the Cape of Good Hope at all costs. Others refer to some terrible crime that was committed on board, or the crew catching the plague and the boat being unable to dock. Some sources point to a seventeenth-century Dutch captain, Bernard Fokke, who sailed so quickly from Holland to Indonesia that he was thought to have sold his soul to the Devil.

Whenever a storm brews off the Cape of Good Hope, it is said that anyone looking into the eye of the storm will see the *Flying Dutchman*.

The officer of the watch of the Royal Navy ship the *Bacchante* described an encounter with the *Flying Dutchman* while rounding the Cape of Good Hope on July 11, 1881: "A strange red light as of a phantom ship all aglow, in the midst of which light the mast, spars and sails of a brig 200 yards distant stood out in strong relief." Soon afterwards, he fell from a mast to his death.

THE KRAKEN

No sea monster was more terrifying than the Kraken. According to legend this enormous, multi-tentacled creature could raise itself out of the water as high as the top of a ship's mast. It would attack a ship and drag it under the water, often splitting the vessel in two, whereupon the crew would drown or be devoured.

The Kraken was described by the famous naturalist Erik Pontoppidan, the Bishop of Bergen, in his *Natural History of Norway* as "the largest and most surprising of all the animal kingdom."

The earliest stories about the Kraken originated in Norway in the twelfth century, and describe a creature the size of an island. The legend is probably grounded in real-life sightings of either a giant octopus or, more likely, a giant squid, which are large enough to wrestle with a sperm whale and have been known to attack ships, probably mistaking them for whales.

THE DEVIL WHALE

The Devil Whale is a huge whale (or a sea turtle in some legends) that resembles an island when it is sleeping, tricking sailors into putting ashore on its back. When they start a fire, the Devil Whale awakes and attacks the ship, dragging it under the water. Early explorer Saint Brendan the Navigator, in his travels, reportedly landed on the back of a Devil Whale on Easter Sunday. As soon as his monks started a fire to cook their meal, the "island" began to swim away, and they quickly scrambled back to their boats.

MERMAIDS

Mermaids had the head and torso of a woman and the tail of a fish. They were thought to sing to sailors and lure them to their deaths, or squeeze the life out of drowning men while they were "rescuing" them. The legend may have arisen from sightings of manatees, large aquatic mammals that carry their young in their arms in the same way a human might carry a baby. A manatee breaking the surface covered in seaweed may have had the appearance of a human form with long flowing tresses. The male equivalent, mermen, had beards, green hair, and a trident; they caused storms and attacked ships. Melusines were nearly identical to mermaids, only they had two tails.

Fictional Pirates

The exploits of pirates made rousing adventure writing, and non-fiction accounts, such as Alexander Exquemelin's *The Buccaneers of America* (1678) and Charles Johnson's *A General History of the Robberies and Murders of the Most Notorious Pyrates* (1724), became bestsellers in their day. Historical pirates also served as the inspiration for fictional counterparts in a number of well-known works of literature.

LONG JOHN SILVER

This fictional creation of Robert Louis Stevenson in his novel *Treasure Island* has remained the iconic romantic image of the pirate ever since its publication in 1883; "His left leg was cut off close by the hip, and under the left shoulder he carried a crutch, which he managed with wonderful dexterity, hopping about upon it like a bird. He was very tall and strong, with a face as big as a ham—plain and pale, but intelligent and smiling." He walked with a parrot perched on his shoulder.

Stevenson based the character of Long John Silver on his friend William Henley, who was described by Stevenson's stepson, Lloyd Osbourne, as "a great, glowing, massive-shouldered fellow with a big red beard and a crutch; jovial, astoundingly clever, and with a laugh that rolled like music; he had an unimaginable fire and vitality; he swept one off one's feet." In one of his letters Stevenson wrote, "I will now make a confession. It was the sight of your [William Henley's] maimed strength and masterfulness that begot Long John Silver . . . the idea of the maimed man, ruling and dreaded by the sound, was entirely taken from you."

Silver is a complex character; he shows himself to be a hard-working, respected, and likeable sailor, and is a father figure to the novel's central protagonist, Jim Hawkins. But he is also a cunning and ruthless pirate, mutineer, and treasure hunter. After Jim Hawkins discovers Captain Flint's treasure map, Silver is hired as the cook aboard the *Hispaniola*, which sets out to locate the booty. However, Silver is actually a pirate. He had been the ship's quartermaster under Captain John Flint and was reputed to have been the only man whom Flint ever feared. He leads a mutiny, but he talks his men into sparing Jim's life. Silver escapes at the end of the book with some of the treasure and is never seen again.

CAPTAIN HOOK

Captain Hook is the pirate villain of J. M. Barrie's play and novel, *Peter Pan*. He was reputed to have been Blackbeard's boatswain and the only man Long John Silver ever feared. He has long black hair, a curly moustache, and his clothing is reminiscent of the elaborate dress of Bartholomew Roberts, although Barrie attributes his appearance to King Charles II.

In place of his right hand, which was cut off by Peter Pan and eaten by a crocodile, he has a fearsome hook. The crocodile follows Hook around, trying to eat him. Hook knows when it is near because it has also swallowed a clock which makes a loud ticking noise.

Hook hates Peter Pan obsessively and spends all his energy trying to kill him and the Lost Boys. At the end of the story he kidnaps Wendy and challenges Peter Pan to a showdown, which he loses, after which he jumps into the jaws of the waiting crocodile rather than surrender.

Some scholars have theorized that Captain Hook was based on Christopher Newport, English Captain of the *Susan Constant*, the ship which carried settlers to Jamestown Colony in Virginia in 1607. Newport also had a metal hook in place of his right hand. Others point to the British explorer Captain James Cook as another possible influence.

CAPTAIN SINGLETON

This fictional creation of Daniel Defoe appeared a year after the success of *Robinson Crusoe*. Like its predecessor, *The Life, Adventures and Piracies of the Famous Captain Singleton* presents a first-person narrative of supposedly factual events.

Bob Singleton is an Englishman who is stolen from a well-to-do family as a child and raised by a sucession of beggars and gypsies. In the first half of the novel he recounts his crossing of Africa, and in the second half he tells of his piracy adventures, although he focuses heavily on economics and logistics rather than the swashbuckling activities usually associated with fictional pirates.

Singleton says of his upbringing, "I had no sense of virtue or religion upon me. I had never heard much of either . . . I was preparing and growing up apace to be as wicked as anybody could be, or perhaps ever was." During his teens he was "perfectly loose and dissolute in my behaviour, bold and wicked while I was under government, and now perfectly unfit to be trusted with liberty, for I was as ripe for any villainy as a young fellow that had no solid thought ever placed in his mind could be supposed to be . . . and all the little scenes of life I had passed through had been full of dangers and desperate circumstances."

Singleton is a hero in the tradition of Bunyan's *Pilgrim's Progress*, an individual beset with challenges seeking salvation in adversity. Like Crusoe, he has to rely on his wits and his ingenuity to survive. He also spends part of his time marooned, on the island of Madagascar.

F L O R I D A P R O
AB INDIGENIS DICTA IAQVAZA

Apalatci

In hoc lacu Indige
argenti ponitu

Oustaca

Onatheaqua

Potanou

Apalou

Ehtamana

Anoiala

Astina

Choin

Vitha

Eloquale

Patchica

Adelano

Chilili

Selanou

Aquouena

Caelica

Calanay

Onnatogno

Mocoso

Coyarca

Onachaquara

Matiacua

Maira

Murracou

Hamocorou

Lacus
aquae dulcis

Adeo magnus est hic lacus
ut ex una ripa conspici altera
non possit. Distat a Charle
fort 180 leucis.

Sorroco

Oathkaqua

Promi. C.

Mocosou

Lacus &
Insula Sarrope

Iari de rex

Astuaria

Binini

B.

Mexicani Sinus pars

Sinus Ioan
nis Ponce

F. Canoci

F. Pacis

Aquatio

CALOS

Calor

Promi.floridae

Iuper

Hac mar

Insula dicta
Testudines

Scopuli dicti
Martyres

Hauana

Iuenos

Cuba insula.

Cuspis S.
Antonij

Xaqua

Guanamarico

Portus
Carenas

Insula
Pinorii

Iardines scopuli, na.
uigantibus formidolosi.

S. Trinitatis.

Pirate Lore

Pirates in real life rarely cut the same swashbuckling figure as the pirates of fiction. The traditional romantic image of the peg-legged pirate captain with a parrot on his shoulder, who left elaborate maps for chests of treasure buried on desert islands, is steeped more in fancy than fact.

TREASURE CHESTS

The ubiquitous iron-banded chest full of pirate treasure owes more to legend than reality. While pirate booty did contain pieces-of-eight, gold, silver, and jewels, most pirate plunder was more mundane. Pirates collected booty that they could eat, drink, or sell quickly rather than hoard, so that their gains could be spent on living the high life. Other pirate "treasure" included fine cloths, spices, baled cotton, salted meat, weapons, ropes, tools, slaves, and, the most popular plunder of all, liquor. All these items would not have been sensibly housed in a wooden chest.

X MARKS THE SPOT: PIRATE MAPS

The pirate map with an X marking the location of buried treasure is one of the most familiar pirate artifacts, but it is a complete fiction created by Robert Louis Stevenson in *Treasure Island*. His stepson, Lloyd Osbourne, described how he was "busy with a box of paints I happened to be tinting a map of an island I had drawn. Stevenson came in as I was finishing it, and with his affectionate interest in everything I was doing, leaned over my shoulder, and was soon elaborating the map and naming it. I shall never forget the thrill of Skeleton Island, Spyglass Hill, nor the heart-stirring climax of the three red crosses! And the greater climax still when he wrote down the words 'Treasure Island' at the top right-hand corner . . . 'Oh, for a story about it,' I exclaimed, in a heaven of enchantment." Within three days Stevenson had completed the opening chapters of his pirate classic.

DESERTED ISLANDS

A desert island is a legitimate part of the pirate lore because marooning was a common punishment for defrauding other pirates of their fair share of spoils, or for desertion. Although fictional accounts of life on a desert island, such as in *Robinson Crusoe*, depict characters adapting to their environment and finding food and shelter, in reality marooning was a virtual death sentence, since many remote islands simply could not sustain human life.

One of the most famous cases of marooning was that of Captain William Greenaway, who, along with seven of his crew, was left on a remote island in the Bahamas when his remaining crew mutinied in 1718. Their ordeal was made worse by the pirates returning several times to hamper their attempts at survival. On the first occasion, the pirates gave the stranded men a sloop, but when they were a mile out from shore they boarded her and slashed the sails. One of the crew had to swim to shore, make a raft, and ferry provisions to the others while they made repairs. Greenaway was finally pressed into service of the pirates, and his marooned men were rescued when the pirates were captured by the Spanish.

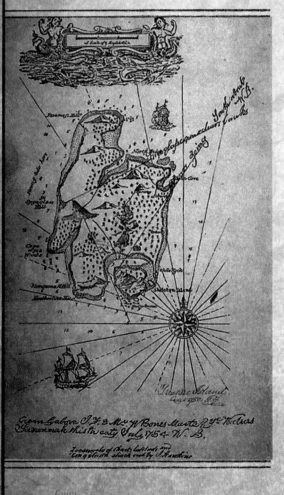

Robinson Crusoe is a fictionalized version of the real-life marooning of Alexander Selkirk who preferred to take his chances on one of the Juan Fernández islands off the coast of Chile rather than travel in what he considered to be William Dampier's unseaworthy ship. He survived on a diet of goats and rats, and dressed himself in goat skins, so that when Dampier returned to the island five years later he was met by a man "who looked wilder than the first owners of them."

SONGS AND SHANTIES

Sea shanties were work songs with rhythms that served more than a social purpose; they helped sailors to synchronize their movements when hauling the sail lines and performing other repetitive tasks, and therefore they were rarely sung ashore. The name comes from the French *chanter* (to sing). They were popular from the fifteenth century until as late as the first half of the twentieth century.

Most shanties have a call-and-response structure, with a lead voice (the shantyman) singing the line, and a chorus of sailors picking up the response. A coordinated pull on the ropes would come on the last syllable of the response.

There are several distinct types of shanty:

✖ **Long-haul shanties:** for rope-pulling tasks that would last a long time. There was often one pull per verse, which allowed men time to pace themselves and recover between pulls

✖ **Short-haul shanties:** for work that involved rapid pulling over short bursts, with two or more pulls per verse

✖ **Halyard shanties:** for more arduous tasks, pulling up and had time between pulls

✖ **Capstan shanties:** the anchor was raised by winding the rope around a huge winch which the sailors turned by walking around it. Since there was no pulling required, these shanties were smoother and had full choruses rather than call and response

✖ **Stamp 'n' go shanties:** on large ships, many men would take hold of a rope and pull on it together tug-of-war style, stamping out the rhythm

✖ **Pumping shanties:** pumping out the bilge hold was a daily chore

✖ **Fo'c's'le shanties:** sea songs with no other function than to have fun. Also known as "forebitters"

The most famous song attributed to pirates was composed by Young E. Allison in 1891, and based on the song in Robert Louis Stevenson's *Treasure Island*. The song is believed to be based on the legend that fifteen mutineers were marooned on Dead Man's Chest Island, in the British Virgin Islands, by the pirate Blackbeard.

"Fifteen Men On A Dead Man's Chest"

Fifteen men on a dead man's chest

Yo ho ho and a bottle of rum

Drink and the devil had done for the rest

Yo ho ho and a bottle of rum

The mate was fixed by the bosun's pike

The bosun brained with a marlinespike

And cookey's throat was marked belike

It had been gripped by fingers ten;

And there they lay, all good dead men

Like break o' day in a boozing ken

Yo ho ho and a bottle of rum!

Fifteen men of the whole ship's list

Yo ho ho and a bottle of rum!

Dead and be damned and the rest gone whist!

Yo ho ho and a bottle of rum!

The skipper lay with his nob in gore

Where the scullion's ax his cheek had shore

And the scullion he was stabbed times four

And there they lay, and the soggy skies

Dripped down in up-staring eyes

In murk sunset and foul sunrise

Yo ho ho and a bottle of rum!

Fifteen men of 'em stiff and stark

Yo ho ho and a bottle of rum!

Ten of the crew had the murder mark!

Yo ho ho and a bottle of rum!

'Twas a cutlass swipe or an ounce of lead

Or a yawing hole in a battered head

And the scuppers' glut with a rotting red

And there they lay, aye, damn my eyes

Looking up at paradise

All souls bound just contrawise

Yo ho ho and a bottle of rum!

Fifteen men of 'em good and true -

Yo ho ho and a bottle of rum!

Ev'ry man jack could ha' sailed with Old Pew,

Yo ho ho and a bottle of rum!

There was chest on chest of Spanish gold

With a ton of plate in the middle hold

And the cabins riot of stuff untold,

And they lay there that took the plum

With sightless glare and their lips struck dumb

While we shared all by the rule of thumb,

Yo ho ho and a bottle of rum!

More was seen through a sternlight screen...

Yo ho ho and a bottle of rum

Chartings undoubt where a woman had been

Yo ho ho and a bottle of rum.

'Twas a flimsy shift on a bunker cot

With a dirk slit sheer through the bosom spot

And the lace stiff dry in a purplish blot

Oh was she wench or some shudderin' maid

That dared the knife and took the blade

By God! she had stuff for a plucky jade

Yo ho ho and a bottle of rum!

Fifteen men on a dead man's chest

Yo ho ho and a bottle of rum

Drink and the devil had done for the rest

Yo ho ho and a bottle of rum.

We wrapped 'em all in a mains'l tight

With twice ten turns of a hawser's bight

And we heaved 'em over and out of sight,

With a Yo-Heave-Ho! and a fare-you-well

And a sudden plunge in the sullen swell

Ten fathoms deep on the road to hell,

Yo ho ho and a bottle of rum!

PEG-LEGS, HOOKS, AND EYEPATCHES

Pirate hooks probably originated with Captain Hook from *Peter Pan*, although some sources believe that J. M. Barrie based the character on Christopher Newport, an English sea captain, who was not a pirate. However, it is certainly true that many pirates lost a hand during battle, so it isn't inconceivable that replacements were fashioned from hooks, though documentary evidence does not back this up.

Leg amputations were also common, but many of these operations would have resulted in the victim bleeding to death or dying from infection. However, the few that survived this ordeal would have fashioned a replacement from available materials on board, such as a piece of timber.

Eyepatches were sometimes used to cover a missing eye, although some people believe that it was used to cover a good eye in order to prepare it for night vision. This intriguing theory is unlikely, since it only takes about thirty minutes for an eye to become accustomed to the dark. Eye injuries were common, and since pirates relied on generating fear in their enemies, it is likely that many of them went into battle with a gaping disfigured socket.

PARROTS

Contrary to romantic mythology, pirates didn't walk around with parrots on their shoulders and rarely kept them as pets. Colorful birds of all species and monkeys were prized pets among the wealthy, but for a pirate they were mostly commodities for sale. A pirate seen around town with a parrot was most likely advertising his wares.

Parrots became linked with pirates in the early 1700s when sailors began returning from the tropics with colorful birds. Parrots were popular because they could be taught to speak, and were easier to transport by ship than other animals.

Some sources argue that pets such as parrots were kept on board as emergency food rations, but there isn't much meat on them and, besides, pirates often operated from island bases, rather than making repeated long voyages.

Parrots were first brought to Europe by the ancient Greeks and Romans. The physician Ctesias describes a plum-headed parakeet at the court of Artaxerxes II and marveled at its ability to mimic speech. By the golden age of piracy, the trade in bringing exotic animals to the courts of Europe was well established. The crowned heads of Europe had their own royal animal collections and this status symbol was emulated by the richest members of the aristocracy, since exotic animals were rare and expensive. It is well known that pirates often dressed like the social and political elite, so it is possible that for some pirates a parrot would have been a prestigious accessory, but the practice was not widespread. Also, a parrot perched on one's shoulder would create quite a mess.

It was Long John Silver and his parrot, Captain Flint, from *Treasure Island*, who firmly melded the image of pirate and parrot in popular romantic lore.

Glossary

Sailing was a highly specialized occupation with its own special language and technical terms. Many modern expressions and phrases can be traced back to maritime language.

abaft/aft towards the rear (stern) of the boat

about the position of a ship after it has tacked

About ship! the order to get ready to tack

adrift at the mercy of the wind and tide; also naval slang for being late or absent from duty

Ahoy! "Attention!"

all standing fully equipped with all sails set; to turn in all standing means to go to sleep fully dressed

amidships midway between the bow and the stern

articles a set of pirate rules to which everyone on board must agree

Arr! "Yes!"

astern the back of or behind the boat

athwart from side to side of a ship; across the length of

Avast! "Stop!"

aweigh the position of the anchor when it has been lifted from the sea bed (hence the expression "anchors aweigh")

bagpipe the mizzen to lay it back by bringing the sheet to the mizzen rigging

batten down to secure hatches and loose objects

beakhead small plank of wood near the bow of the uppermost deck with holes cut for defecation

belay to secure or make fast a rope by winding it around a cleat or pin

below beneath the top deck

binnacle a box located near the helm that houses and protects the compass

binnacle list the ship's sick list, kept in the binnacle

bitter end the last part of a rope or chain

black spot a pirate death threat, involving handing your enemy a piece of paper with a black spot on it, often with more specific details written on the other side. This practice is featured in *Treasure Island*

blunt slang word for money; thought to refer to the rounded edges of minted coins

bow the front section of a ship or boat; the oar or the rower closest to the bow

bowsprit a large piece of timber extending forward from the stem of a ship, to which the stays of the foremast are fastened

brig-rigged a ship with fore-and-aft rigging on the mizzenmast, and square-rigging on the foremast and/or mainmast

broadside the simultaneous firing of all the guns on one side of a ship

buccaneer pirates who operated mostly in the Spanish Main in the seventeenth century; named for the original French settlers of the region who made their living *boucanning* (smoking meat)

Cape Horn fever an illness feigned to shirk duties

captain's daughter another name for the cat-o'-nine-tails

careen to turn the ship upside down and clean the seaweed and barnacles from the hull

cat-o'-nine-tails a hemp or leather whip with nine lashes, each finished with three blood knots; used for flogging

crimp a swindler; also a member of the naval press gang

cut and run cut the anchor rope and run before the wind; to make a quick getaway

cut of your jib a person's demeanor and conduct

dead lights eyes

dead men empty bottles, because the "spirit" has left them; hence "down among the dead men let him lie"

dogwatch two periods of evening watch duty, from four to six, and from six to eight. Dogwatch is either a corruption of "dodge watch" or is associated with the fitful sleep of sailors known as dog sleep

doubloon an old Spanish gold coin equivalent to sixteen pieces-of-eight (128 reales)

draft the depth of water a boat draws

even keel a keel that is parallel with the horizon

fathom a nautical unit of length equal to approximately six feet. When drawing up the anchor line, it was roughly the distance between the tips of index fingers of both hands, with arms outstretched

flash in the pan something of promise that yields nothing; derived from the failure of gunpowder ignited in a flintlock pistol's priming pan to set off a charge

fore-and-aft rigged hanging sails from spars attached to the main-mast

foremast the front mast of a three-masted ship

fouled a piece of equipment that is jammed, tangled, or ruined

French leave a temporary leave of absence taken with the intention of returning

futtock shrouds iron rods extending from the lower mast to brace the base of the topmast

galley the kitchen

grommet an apprentice sailor, or ship's boy; from the Spanish word *grumete*

gunwale the upper edge of the side of a boat

going on the account slang term a captain used to let it be known he was looking for voluntary recruits for a pirating expedition

half-cocked refers to the practice of keeping a flintlock pistol partially cocked; "going off half-cocked" is slang for an unexpected outburst

hearties those with heart; brave and loyal comrades

heave ahead to move forward by heaving in the rope fastened to an anchor some distance away in front of the ship

heave astern to move backwards by heaving in the rope fastened to an anchor some distance away astern the ship

heave to to bring the ship to a halt by setting the sails against each other so they cancel out

hornswoggler a cheat or liar

Jolly Roger the traditional pirate flag featuring skull and crossbones

junk old bits of rope; also slang term for salt meat

keelhauling a severe punishment involving drawing a person under the keel

kiss the wooden lady a punishment in which a sailor hugs the mast and has his hands lashed together

Land ho! "I can see land!"

landfall the first land sighted after a sea voyage

landlubber a clumsy seaman, or a person unfamiliar with the sea or seamanship

lateen sails triangular sails that allowed a ship to sail in a direction other than that of the wind

lee the side away from the direction from which the wind blows; the side sheltered from the wind

leeway the sideways movement of the boat

Letter of Marque a document issued by a government authorizing a private citizen to attack enemy ships and goods

letting the cat out of the bag Navy reference to the custom of keeping the cat-o'-nine-tails in a bag tied to the mast; sailors fearful of a flogging dreaded "letting the cat out of the bag"

lower mast the lower of three levels for hanging a sail from the yard-arm of a square-rigged ship

lubber a clumsy oaf

luff setting the helm towards the lee side of the ship to sail closer to the wind; the forward side of a fore-and-aft sail

mainmast the middle mast on a three-masted ship, and front mast on a two-masted ship

magazine the ship's gunpowder store

make land to discover land from afar

mastheading punishment involving forcing someone to the highest part of the ship's mast, often during bad weather

mizzenmast the rear mast on a three-masted ship

monkey small cannon

motley crew slang term for groups of idiosyncratically dressed pirates

no quarter given surrendering will lead to being spared, but resistance means death

oggin the sea

piece of eight an old Spanish silver coin worth eight reales; the coin could be cut into pieces to make lower denominations

point blank the distance a shot travels before it falls significantly below the horizontal plane of the bore

powder monkey the sailor (often a boy) who supplies the gunners with powder

press gang gangs of wharf laborers employed by the Impress Service of the Royal Navy to forcibly recruit sailors

privateer pirates who contracted and shared plunder with their governments

purser rigged and parish damned a term applied to men joining the navy to escape troubles on land

Ready About! a command instructing the crew to be attentive and prepare for tacking

run a rig to play a trick

savvy "Do you understand?" from the French *savoir*

scud to run before a gale with little or no sail set

scuppers drain holes in the side of a ship at deck level to allow water to run off

scuttle to intentionally sink

scuttlebutt gossip or rumor; sailors would gather and talk the ship's water butt in which a hole would be drilled (the butt was scuttled) to release the liquid

sea dog derogatory slang for a seasoned sailor, until Queen Elizabeth II used the phrase to mean privateers who bravely defended British interests

set sail to spread out the sails to the wind in order to start moving

shipboard articles of conduct a set of rules some pirates compelled captives to sign when forcing them to join on with their crews

ship shape and Bristol fashion the ship is ready to sail and all the equipment is stowed securely; the port of Bristol has one of the most variable tidal flows in the world, so prior to the construction of a floating harbor in 1803, all goods needed to be securely stowed for moored ships to withstand being beached there at low tide

ship-rigged a ship whose masts are all square-rigged

shiver me timbers an expression of surprise, referring to artillery fire exploding wood on a ship into flying "shivers," or long splinters

shorten sail to bring in some of the sail to slow the ship, or as a safety precaution during bad weather

skedaddle to slink away from a working party or the scene of battle

sloop-rigged a ship with fore-and-aft rigging on all masts

square-rigged hanging sails from the yardarms

strike colors to surrender by lowering the ship's flag

swab a rope-yarn mop for cleaning decks; also a term of contempt

swallow the anchor to retire from sailing

taking the king's shilling the practice of paying a shilling to recruits who enlisted in the Navy

top-gallant the highest of three levels to hang a sail from the yardarm of a square-rigged ship

topmast the mast level above the lower mast on a square-rigged ship

tricorne the traditional three-cornered hat sported by pirates

trysail a special sail hung from the lower mast of a square-rigged ship during a storm to stabilize the vessel and make it less likely to capsize

weigh anchor to lift the anchor from the sea floor in preparation for sailing

wind's eye the direction from which the wind blows; a person facing the wind is looking into the wind's eye

yardarm long pieces of timber, tapering towards the ends, hung by the center horizontally across and at right-angles to (athwart) the mast, to support sails and rigging

You scratch my back, I'll scratch yours a phrase that has its origins in a private agreement between two sailors to deliver light blows during a flogging; scratching the skin drew blood, making the wounds appear worse than they were

F L O R I D A   P R O

AB INDIGENIS DICTA IAQVAZA

Hic defendit
Pamphilus Naruaez.

Sinus Magnus

Vitra

Eloquale

Aquouna
Cadica
Mocofo
Mathiaca

Maira

Lacus
aquæ dulcis

Adeo magnus est hic lacus
ut ex vna ripa conspici altera
non possit. Distat a Charles
fort 180 leucis.

M E X I C A N I   S I N V S   pars

Sinus Ioan
nis Ponce.

F. Canoes

F. Pacis

Aquatio

C A L O S

Calos

Insula dictæ
Testudines.

Scopuli dicti
Martyres

Lacus &
Insula Sarrope

Iart de Ines

Æstuaria

Bimini

Bahi

Prom: Florida.

Haec maris

Rupes

Oustaca

Onatheaquia

Potanu

Ehiamana

Anouala
Hica
Astina

Chozi

Puchita
Edelano
Chilili
Calanay

Onataqua
Onachaquana

Mayarca

Mirracou

Hanouo vous
coru

Sorroci

Sorrocha

Prom: Canc

M.Ocosson

M.Ocosson

Oathkaqua

In hoc lacu Indigene
argenti grana r

A palata

A c.
Hauana

Portus
Matahaica

C u b a   i n s u l a.

Cuspis. S.
Antonij

Nanguc

Guanaynarico

Insula
Pinorii

Iardines scopuli, na=
uiganubus formidabiles.

S. Trinitatis

Mexicani Sinus pars